Computer problem solving

made easy

Which? Books are commissioned and published by Which? Ltd,
2 Marylebone Road, London NW1 4DF
Email: books@which.co.uk

British Library Cataloguing in Publication Data
A catalogue record for this book is available from the British Library

Picture credits:
Microsoft product screen shot(s) reprinted with permission from Microsoft
Corporation. All other pictures courtesy of Microsoft except for pages 170, 173
and 174, which contain images courtesy of Lynn Wright, and pages 83, 84 and 175,
courtesy of Lynn Wright.
Microsoft, Encarta, MSN, and Windows are either registered trademarks or
trademarks of Microsoft Corporation in the United States and/or other countries.
Adobe product screenshot(s) reprinted with permission from Adobe Systems
Incorporated.

ISBN 978 1 84490 145 6

1 3 5 7 9 10 8 6 4 2

Consultant editor: Lynn Wright
Project manager: Emma Callery
Designer: Blanche Williams, Harper Williams Ltd
Proofreader: Kathy Steer
Indexer: Christine Bernstein
Printed and bound by Charterhouse, Hatfield
Distributed by Littlehampton Book Services Ltd, Faraday Close, Durrington,
Worthing, West Sussex BN13 3RB

Essential Velvet is an elemental chlorine-free paper produced at Condat in Périgord,
France using timber from sustainably managed forests. The mill is ISO14001 and
EMAS certified.

For a full list of Which? Books, please call 01903 828557 or access our website at
www.which.co.uk/books, or write to Littlehampton Book Services.

Computer problem solving

made easy

Contents

Windows 7 problems

Email and communication

Internet and web problems

Home working

Photos, music and video

Syncing problems

Essential advice

Resources

Editorial note

The instructions in this guide refer to the Windows 7 operating system. Where other software or websites are mentioned, instructions refer to the latest versions (at the time of going to print). If you have a different version, the steps may vary slightly.

Screenshots are used for illustrative purposes only.

Windows 7 is an American product. All spellings on the screenshots and on the buttons and boxes in the text are therefore spelled in US English. The rest of the text remains in UK English.

All technical words in the book are either discussed in jargon busters within the text and/or can be found in the Jargon buster section on page 216.

Introduction

Computers can be fickle devices. When they work well, they can save you time, money and open up a world of connectivity and creativity. But when your computer is playing up, you could end up stumped by a problem that seems impossible to fix. That's where *Computer Problem Solving Made Easy* can help.

Packed with step-by-step instructions, it offers plain English advice to solve all manner of PC problems – from common annoyances to full-blown emergencies. Each step includes clear images to help you follow the text, and informative tips and advice to help you solve your particular computing conundrum. All the advice is backed up with a comprehensive jargon buster starting on page 216 to explain obscure computer terminology.

A companion book to *PC Problem Solving Made Easy* (see below), this useful volume will help you to solve another wide range of common computer challenges. From Windows 7-specific issues, such as start-up and shut-down problems, to speeding up a sluggish PC, through to essential advice on backing-up and recovering a PC from a disaster. This book also covers everyday computing errors that you will face. From fixing Facebook and tweaking Twitter troubles, to sorting out Skype video-calling problems, our guide will keep you connected. And if you use your PC for work, frustrating problems posed by Microsoft Word 2010 and Excel 2010 can be solved. There is even advice on sorting out syncing problems when you connect your iPod, iPad or iPhone, through to getting on top of music, video and photo problems.

Computer Problem Solving Made Easy aims to quickly and easily get your computer back up and running, taking the stress out of PC problem solving and putting you back in charge of your computer.

To purchase our book *PC Problem Solving Made Easy* (RRP £10.99 ISBN: 978-1-84490-109-8) visit www.which.co.uk/books or call 01903 828557. The book is also available from all good book shops.

Windows 7 problems

By reading this chapter you'll get to grips with:

- Fixing common start-up and shut-down issues
- Speeding up your PC
- Solving printing problems

Start-up issues

Over a period of time, some PCs can become noticeably slower when you switch them on from being shut down. This can be frustrating, taking minutes for Windows 7 to be ready to use. The problem is that over time, Windows 7 PCs can become laden with start-up files, incorrect settings and digital garbage that clogs up your PC. Here are a few problem-solving steps to speed up start-up times.

My computer is taking a long time to start up

As you install applications, many add small settings and programs to your computer's start-up process. It's a good idea to remove as many unneeded start-up items as possible.

1 To show what programs run at start-up, click **Start** and type **msconfig** in the search box. In the results panel above the search box, click the program **msconfig**.

2 The 'System Configuration' window will appear (see Be Careful!, opposite). Click the **Startup** tab. This shows a list of all programs and items that start when you turn on your PC. The more unneeded items you have in the list, the longer your computer can take to start.

3 Untick the check box next to any items you don't want to run at start-up. If in doubt what to choose, pick items that share the names of applications you never or rarely use. In this example, 'Skype' and 'Roxio Burn' are unticked.

4 Click **Apply**, then click **OK** to dismiss the 'System Configuration' window. Click **Start**, then click the 'Shutdown' **arrow**, and choose **Restart** from the pop-up menu. Your PC will now restart without the start-up items you unticked loading.

Help! I keep launching the wrong software

Windows 7 tries to keep things simple by hiding the extension of files, and by automatically launching what it thinks is the best application for the file you're trying to open when you double click on it. Most of the time that's fine, but without extensions showing, it's easy to inadvertently launch the wrong application. Here are ways to help you avoid doing this:

Show hidden extensions

1 Click **Start**, then click **Computer**.

2 In the window that appears, click **Organize** in the menu bar, and from the drop-down menu select **Folder and search options**.

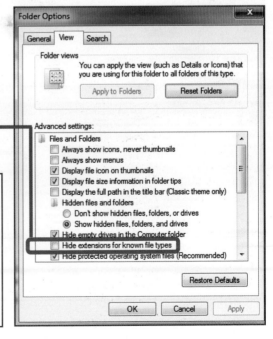

Folder and search options

3 In the 'Folder Options' dialog box, click the **View** tab.

4 Under 'Advanced settings:', untick the check box next to 'Hide extensions for known file types'. You will now be able to judge what application a file will launch by its extension name. A file ending in .docx will open in Microsoft Word, for example.

☐ Hide extensions for known file types

BE CAREFUL!

System Configuration (MSConfig) is a powerful program suited to advanced users – and unticking the wrong start-up item can cause your PC to behave oddly. If in doubt, untick a start-up item, then restart your PC following Step 4 opposite. If it behaves oddly, then follow the process described, but make sure you place a tick next to the start-up item that caused problems when it was prevented from running at start-up so that it runs at start-up in the future.

Determine which files should open in which application

Some file types, such as picture files (an example would be a file ending in .jpg), can be opened in many different programs that are installed on your PC. The trouble is that when you click on a type of file you want to open in one program, Windows 7 opens it in the wrong one. Here's how to fix it:

1 Click **Start**, then click **Control Panel**.

2 Click **Programs**.

3 Under the 'Default Programs' heading, click on the **Make a file type always open in a specific program** link.

4 In the 'Set Associations' dialog box, scroll down the list until you see the file extension that you want to change the default program for.

5 Click on the **file** extension to highlight it and then click **Change program...**.

6 In the 'Open With' dialog box, click the program you wish to make the default program for that file type. If you can't see it listed here under 'Recommended Programs', click **Browse** to find the program on your computer.

7 Click **OK** to apply your changes. Click **Close** and then the red **X** icon to exit the 'Control Panel'.

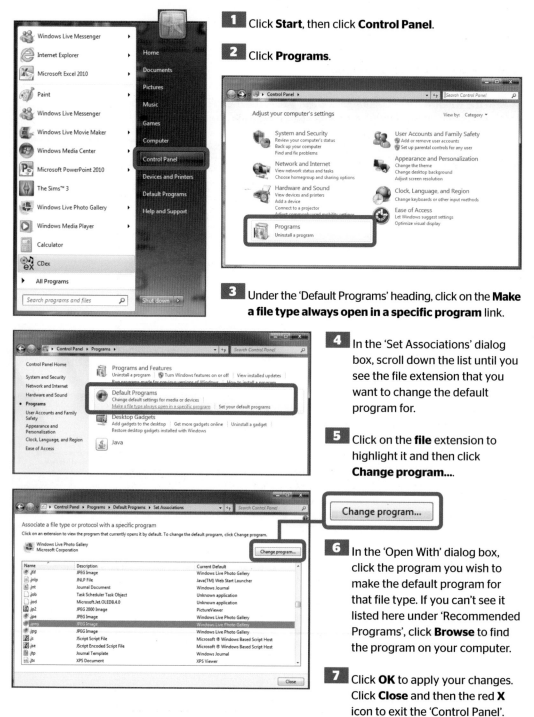

Shut-down problems

Many people encounter problems with Windows shutting down without warning. It can be very annoying when this happens as potentially you can lose work if you haven't saved recently.

Windows 7 keeps shutting down randomly

While it's hard to pinpoint the exact cause of random Windows 7 shutdowns, here are few things you can try.

Stop Windows updating automatically

Windows 7 includes automatic downloading and installing of updates and fixes so your PC is always running as smoothly as possible. Sometimes, Windows 7 needs to reboot when it has installed an update, and it can do this automatically and without warning. To change this:

1 Click **Start**, then click **Control Panel**. Click **System and Security**.

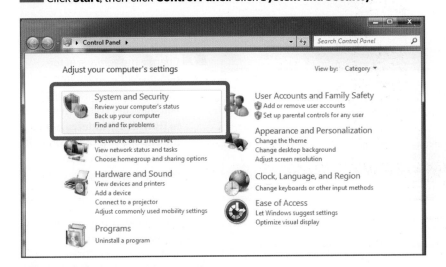

2 Click **Windows Update**.

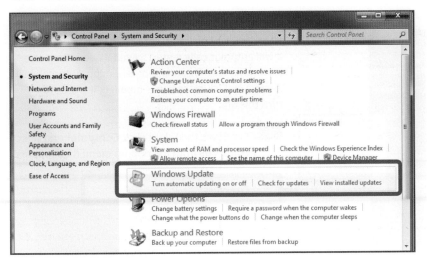

3 In the left-hand sidebar of the 'Windows Update' window, click the **Change settings** button.

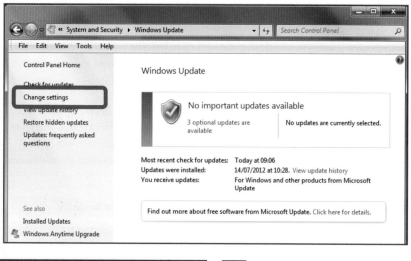

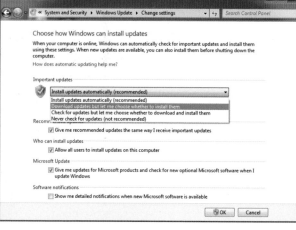

4 Change the settings of the pop-up menu under 'Important Updates' from 'Install updates automatically (recommended)' to **Download updates but let me choose whether to install them**. Click **OK** to apply the new settings.

Now when new updates for Windows 7 are available, they'll be downloaded and you will be asked if you want them installed. Once installed, Windows 7 will restart – but this time you will have advanced notice.

Turn off automatic restart

Sometimes when things go wrong with Windows 7, it will automatically restart – even if everything else is working fine. This happens when the 'Automatically Restart on Failure' option is enabled. It is safe to turn this off.

1 Click **Start**, then right click **Computer** and select **Properties** from the pop-up menu that appears.

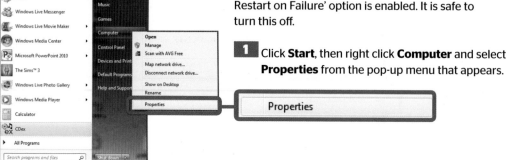

2 In the 'System' window and in the left-hand sidebar, click **Advanced system settings**.

3 In the 'System Properties' dialog box, under 'Startup and Recovery', click **Settings...**.

4 In the 'Startup and Recovery' dialog box, untick the option 'Automatically restart', then click **OK**.

5 Click **Apply**, then click **OK** in the 'System Properties' window.

Now when your computer experiences a problem, such as a program crashing, it won't automatically restart and it will give you a warning – and the opportunity to save your work.

Clean your registry

One of the main culprits behind random Windows shutdowns, is a problem with the system registry. The registry co-ordinates all the settings from Windows 7 and the programs you run, and if any of these settings gets corrupted, it can make Windows 7 crash and restart. By cleaning your registry you can resolve issues.

> **Jargon buster**
> **System registry** A central database used by Windows to store information about user preferences, installed software, hardware and drivers, and other settings needed for the operating system to run correctly.

1 One of the best free applications for cleaning the registry is CCleaner. Open your web browser, and type **www.piriform.com/ccleaner** into the address bar.

2 Press **Enter** and then click the green **Download** button on the web page. In the page that appears, download the 'CCleaner Free' edition.

3 Follow the download and installation instructions, and complete the software installation.

4 Click **Start**, then click **All Programs** and click the **CCleaner** folder. In the folder, click the **CCleaner** application to launch it.

5 In the CCleaner interface, click the **Registry** icon, then click the **Scan for Issues** button to run a system scan. You see a long list of problems, with all of them automatically selected.

6 Click the **Fix selected issues...** and click **Yes** to the 'Do you want to backup changes to the registry?' warning box that appears. It will prompt you for a location to save the backup file – find a suitable location anywhere on your hard disk (in this case, the Documents library), then click **Save**.

7 Once saved, you are presented with a window detailing the problems with each registry item. You can use the arrow buttons to examine each one, but as you backed up the registry in step 6, you can click the **Fix All Selected Issues** button.

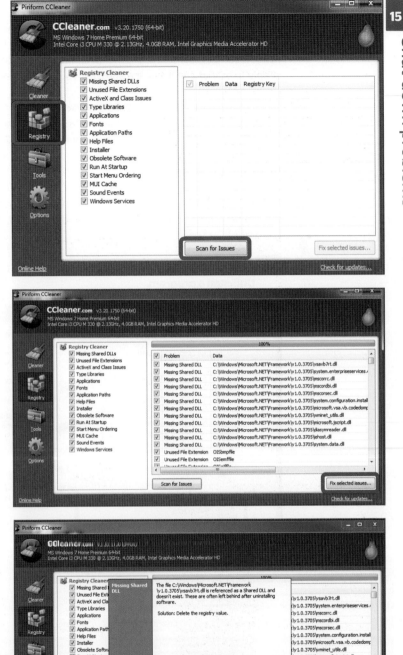

8 The registry is now cleaned of problem files. Click **Close** and then exit CCleaner.

Computer performance

A sluggish computer is one of the most common problems faced by PC users. Not only is it frustrating having to wait for a computer to finish the task you set it, but it can be a symptom of other problems. The good news is there are some simple fixes that can boost the speed of your computer.

My computer is running too slowly

Try the problem solving steps given on pages 16-24 and then if you still have no success, try out the further ideas described on pages 24-6.

Uninstall unused programs

Unused or forgotten programs installed on your computer can slow down your PC by clogging up its hard disk and by running tasks in the background. If there are any programs on your PC that you no longer need, uninstall them to help give your PC a speed bump.

1 Click **Start**, then click **Control Panel** and then in the 'Programs' box, click **Uninstall a program**.

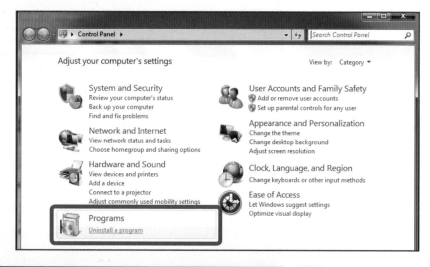

2 In the 'Uninstall or change a program' window, all the programs installed on your computer are listed. Click the **Organize** button, point to 'Layout' and click on **Menu bar**. A menu will appear at the top of the window.

3 Select the **View** menu, then point to 'Sort by' and click on **More...**.

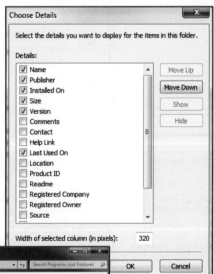

4 In the 'Choose Details' window that appears, click the box next to 'Last Used On'. Click **OK**.

5 In the 'Uninstall or change a program' window, you can sort the list of programs installed on your computer by 'Last used' or by 'Installed on' and other criteria by clicking on the column header text.

6 Scan through the list of programs, identifying any that you no longer use. Click on a program you want to remove, then click **Uninstall/Change**. Follow the on-screen instructions to complete the process

Turn off the Windows Sidebar and Gadgets

Windows 7 allows you to have small always-on applets known as 'Desktop Gadgets' running in the background on your desktop at all times. These can sap power and slow down your computer, so it's worth turning them all off if you need a speed boost.

1 Click **Start**, then click **Control Panel**. In the search box in the upper-right corner of the 'Control Panel' window, type features. In the resulting window under 'Programs and Features' click **Turn Windows features on or off**.

2 In the 'Windows Features' window that appears, clear the tick box next to 'Windows Gadget Platform', then click **OK**. All the gadgets will disappear from the desktop. To turn them back on again at a later date, follow the two steps, but click on the tick box next to 'Windows Gadget Platform'.

3 Alternatively, if you want to just close a few Desktop Gadgets, move your mouse over a Desktop Gadget, and click the white **X** that appears in the upper-right of the gadget.

Jargon buster

Applets A small application, such as a utility program, that performs one or two simple tasks.

Windows Gadgets A small application that sits on the desktop and performs a simple function, such as displaying the time or the weather.

Install the latest Windows updates

Microsoft periodically releases Windows updates. These are important because they often patch security flaws, but they can sometimes address performance issues too, fixing problems that were slowing down your computer.

1 Click **Start** and type **updates** in the search box. Click on the **Windows Updates** link that appears.

2 Click on **Check for updates** on the left for the latest updates, or click on **Change settings**. Change the settings of the pop-up menu under 'Important updates' and ensure that **Download updates but let me choose whether to install them** is selected.

> Windows Update
>
> **Control Panel Home**
> Check for updates
> Change settings
> View update history
> Restore hidden updates
> Updates: frequently asked questions
>
> See also
> Installed Updates
> Windows Anytime Upgrade
>
> Checking for updates...
>
> Most recent check for updates: Yesterday at 17:04
> Updates were installed: Today at 11:07 (Failed).
> View update history
> You receive updates: For Windows and other products from Microsoft Update
>
> Find out more about free software from Microsoft Update.
> Click here for details.

If there are any new updates, these will be downloaded if your computer is connected to the internet, then Windows will ask if you want to install them.

Limit start-up programs

Many applications you install will configure themselves to run whenever you start Windows. In the case of your anti-virus or security software, this is a good thing. But limiting the number of other programs that attempt to launch at startup will speed up Windows and give you a much better all-round performance.

A quick way to check what start-up programs you have running is to check your 'Notification Area', located at the bottom right of the Taskbar. This shows a series of icons and clicking on the arrow will display more.

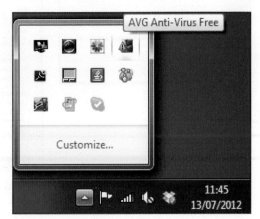

1 Position the mouse cursor over an icon. Windows will display the name of the program it belongs to.

2 If you don't need them to launch at startup consider disabling them. See page 8 for more detailed instructions on disabling start-up programs, including hidden programs.

Clean up your hard disk

Freeing up hard disk space can dramatically help to speed up a slow PC, and you can use Windows' 'Disk Cleanup' tool included in Windows 7 to safely delete unnecessary temporary files.

1 Click **Start**, then click **Computer**. In the pop-up window, right click on the system drive (it will typically be labelled 'OS (C:)', and show a hard drive icon with a small Windows logo) and select **Properties** from the pop-up menu.

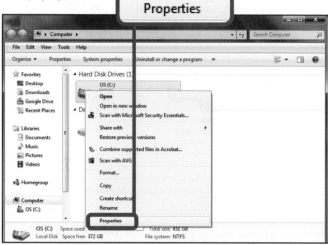

2 Click the **General** tab, and then click on the **Disk Cleanup** button.

3 If prompted, select the 'all users' option. Windows will calculate how much space can be freed up and show a list of files that can be safely removed from the PC. It's safe to tick all of the items here, though you can uncheck any you'd prefer not to delete. Click **OK**, then **Delete Files**.

Keep the desktop tidy

Another often overlooked way to speed up your PC, particularly at startup, is to spend a bit of time tidying up your desktop. Most of us dump loads of files and shortcuts on our desktop until it becomes cluttered with dozens of icons. But your PC has to refresh these icons every so often and this can cause a temporary slowdown.

Rather than delete them all, create a single folder on your desktop called, for example, 'My Icons'. To do this, right click the desktop, point to 'New' and then click **Folder**. Using the mouse, drag the icons into the new folder.

Cut down on visual effects

The graphical effects that make Windows look pretty can also drain resources and slow down your machine. Disabling them might make your desktop look a little drab, but can give you a big speed boost.

1 Right click on an empty area of your desktop and select **Personalize**.

2 Scroll down and select **Windows 7 Basic**. This will turn off most of the snazzy effects. Select **Windows Classic** for even more of a speed boost.

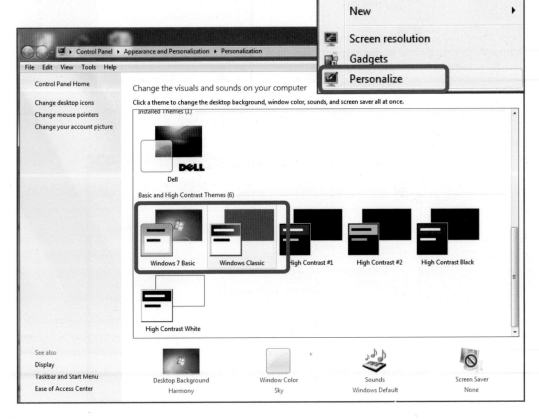

Defragment your hard disk

Your PC can become slower as data on your hard disk becomes fragmented over time – files are split into smaller pieces and stored in different locations on your hard drive. When the computer needs to read a fragmented file, it has to access several locations on the disk, which is a lot slower if the file is stored entirely in a single location.

1 Click **Start**, then click **All Programs**. From the list that appears, click the **Accessories** folder, and then click **System Tools** followed by **Disk Defragmenter**.

2 The 'Disk Defragmenter' dialog lists all the hard drives connected to your computer, including internal ones, along with a percentage figure according to the fragmentation status of that disk.

3 Select the disk you want to defragment, then click the **Defragment disk** button in the lower-right of the window and follow the on-screen prompts.

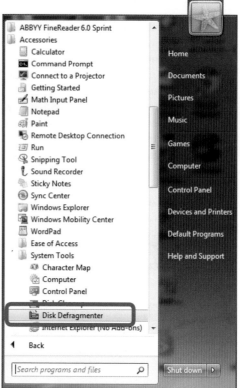

Increase your performance

Many computers - especially laptops - are configured to reduce the performance where possible in order to save on power consumption and lengthen battery time. But if your laptop is plugged into the mains or you're not worried about how quickly your battery drains, you can speed up your PC by adjusting the computer's power options.

1 Click **Start**, then click **Control Panel**. In the window that appears, click **Hardware and Sound**.

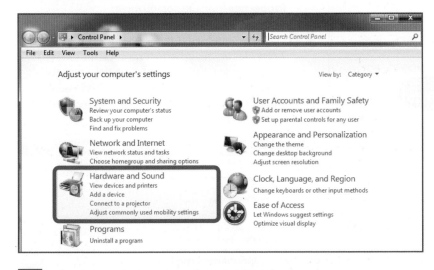

2 In the new window that appears, click **Power Options**. A window will appear titled 'Select a power plan' and listing several power plans. Click the 'Show additional plans' **drop-down arrow**.

3 Click the **selection circle** next to the 'High performance' option. This will give you the maximum speed from your computer, though your laptop battery will drain faster if you're not plugged into the mains.

Change indexing options

Windows creates an index on your hard disk to help speed up the time it takes to find a file you're searching for. But indexing can slow down your computer, so it's worth considering disabling this feature if your computer is dragging its heels.

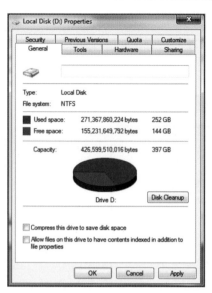

1 Click **Start**, then click **Computer**. In the window that appears, right click on the **system drive** (it will typically be labelled 'OS (C:)', and show a hard drive icon with a small Windows logo) and select **Properties** from the pop-up menu.

2 Click the **General** tab, then untick the box next to 'Allow files on this drive to have contents indexed in addition to file properties'. Click **OK** and in the confirmation box, make sure the option to apply changes to subfolders and files is selected, and then click **OK**.

PC changes to combat slow-down

If you've tried to fix a slow PC with the steps on pages 16–24 and it is still sluggish, there are extra steps you can take – including switching software, adding memory or examining devices – that can also solve the problem. Here are some extra fixes for a slow computer.

Switch to a faster browser

The speed with which you're able to browse web pages is largely down to how fast your broadband connection is. But it's possible to make a significant speed increase by switching to a faster web browser.

If you're still using an older version of Internet Explorer to view web pages, for example, then you will almost certainly notice a big difference by upgrading to the latest version, Internet Explorer 9 (http://windows.microsoft.com/en-us/internet-explorer/products/ie/home).

Consider switching to Firefox (www.mozilla.com/firefox) or Google Chrome (www.google.com/chrome) instead, as a different browser may give your web browsing a boost. As they're free, they're worth testing out.

Get an easy memory boost

A quick way to get a speed boost on Windows 7 is to use a USB memory drive, which adds extra memory to your computer in a similar way to adding more RAM. The drive must be larger than 256MB and conform to Windows data read/write speed requirements.

1 Plug in the USB memory drive, and select the **Speed up my system** option from the AutoPlay menu that appears. Windows will test the device's suitability and, if it passes muster, click on the **ReadyBoost** tab in the dialog box that will open up.

2 Select 'Speed up my system using Windows ReadyBoost' and adjust the slider to select how much free space you want to assign to ReadyBoost. The remaining space can be used for storage as normal. Click **OK** to finish.

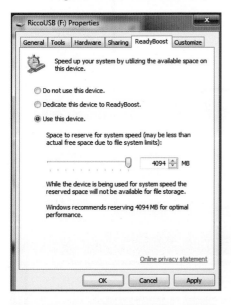

Your computer will use the USB drive as additional computer memory, helping speed up how quickly it works. It isn't as good as adding physical RAM memory, but it's handy as a quick fix.

> ### Jargon buster
> **ReadyBoost** A Windows feature that lets you add memory to a system using flash memory, such as a USB drive, to improve performance without having to add additional system memory.

Unplug USB devices and remove discs

External drives, devices and discs can all slow down the performance of your computer. For instance, when your computer starts it will always check to see if there's a CD or DVD in your drive. If there is, it will take extra time to spin the disc up and identify it. Similarly, power and other system resources can be drained by an external USB drive. Even printers, wi-fi adapters and TV cards can sap performance if they're plugged in.

To maximise your PC's speed potential, unplug all but the most essential devices from USB sockets and make sure you eject any CDs or DVDs when you're finished with them.

Use CCleaner to give your PC a spring clean

As you use your computer, settings get corrupted, files broken and data that's no longer needed can clog up the system. It's a complex task to fix all this, but free system cleaning tools such as CCleaner can handle the hard work for you.

1 Download CCleaner following steps 1–4 on page 14 to download, install and launch it.

2 In the CCleaner interface click the **Analyze** button to run a system scan – be warned that this can take a while to run. You get a long list of files that are no longer being used by Windows 7 and the programs you have running on it, with all of them automatically selected.

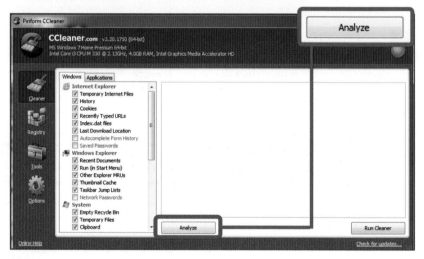

3 Click the **Run Cleaner** button to clean out all those unwanted files, get some spare hard drive space back and speed up your PC.

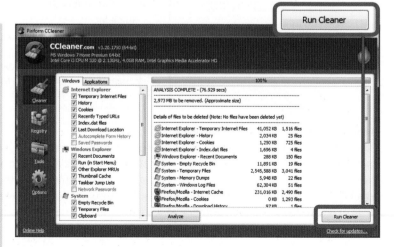

Tip

Software running in the background can have a big impact on your PC's speed, and one of the biggest culprits is security software. While individual security software can vary, it's worth looking through the program's settings and reducing the number of scheduled scans. Alternatively, switch to a less resource-hungry brand of security software – Which? reviews has up-to-date tests of all the latest security programs.

Computer rescue

If you choose to have a cup of tea, glass of water or bottle of wine while using your laptop, you run the risk of possible liquid damage to your PC.

Help! I've spilled water on my laptop

Spilling liquid onto your keyboard or laptop doesn't mean your laptop is ruined – but you must act quickly to minimise damage. The steps below are primarily to rescue a laptop, but will work with a keyboard plugged into a desktop PC as well.

1 Power down the laptop as soon as possible. If you're working on a crucial document, save it immediately, then hold down the power key for around five seconds and the computer will shut all power off. If the laptop is running off a cable from the mains, make sure you turn it off at the wall before you remove the power lead.

2 As quickly as possible turn the laptop upside down to stop the water going further into the machine. By opening the laptop out and sitting it on a flat surface as an upside-down V, you can prevent the computer or the screen from further water damage.

3 Remove the laptop battery as detailed in the manufacturer's manual. This will prevent liquid from reaching the battery unit and potentially causing an electrical hazard. Don't attempt to do this until after you have unplugged the laptop from the mains.

4 Take out any devices that may be attached to the laptop such as USB dongles and SD cards. Also if you are able to remove the keyboard from the laptop, remove this and clean off any water.

> ### Jargon buster
> **USB dongle** Any small USB device – such as a USB drive or 3G broadband device – that plugs into the USB port of your laptop.
> **SD card** A small media card that stores data – SD cards are used by digital cameras and camcorders to store photos or video.

Dealing with a serious spill

If you're quick and the spill is small, then simply allowing the laptop or keyboard to dry could fix the problem. For a more serious spillage:

1 Follow steps 1–4 above, then open up the casing of your laptop, as detailed in the manufacturer's manual, using a small screwdriver for electronic components. Then use a lint-free towel to mop up as much of the spillage as possible. **WARNING:** Do not attempt this before removing the battery and ensuring the laptop is not plugged into the mains.

2 Using the screwdriver, remove the hard drive and memory from the laptop (as detailed in the manufacturer's manual) before water reaches them. If they're wet, place them on dry kitchen towels and allow them to dry.

3 Leave your laptop and all the components for 48 hours in a cool dry place, allowing air to get to as much of the laptop as possible.

4 Return the components to the laptop and test it out. I hopefully these steps have been enough to save your equipment, but if your laptop or keyboard is non-responsive, all hope isn't lost – a reputable PC technician may still be able to save it.

Laptop issues

Small and lightweight with a built-in screen and keyboard, laptops are a great alternative to desktop computers. They offer a powerful performance combined with ability to carry and use them wherever you go. However, as a laptop user you may face some specific laptop problems such as battery life issues.

My laptop battery drains too quickly

Few things are more annoying than the battery low alert popping up on your laptop when you least expect it. Funny how it always happens at the worst possible time – in the middle of finishing an important document, for instance, or perhaps while booking those airline tickets online for your winter sun. Here are some easy fixes that will extend your battery:

Lower screen brightness

The most effective way to reduce the rate of your battery's power consumption is to lower the brightness of your laptop's screen. Brightness keys are typically one of the Function keys found along the top of your keyboard. They usually have a small icon of a sun on them, along with an arrow pointing up or down. To lower your screen's brightness, you will need to repeatedly press the Function key with a sun icon and down arrow.

Switch off wi-fi and Bluetooth

Another way to save power is to switch off wi-fi when you're not using it, as leaving your connection on can sap battery life. As with brightness controls, most laptops have a dedicated switch or a Function key that can be used to disable or enable wi-fi. Check for a button labelled 'wi-fi' or one with an icon that looks either like a radio mast or like the signal bars on a mobile phone. Bluetooth is also worth keeping an eye on, as it's often on even when it is never used.

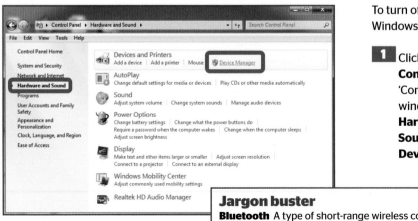

To turn off Bluetooth in Windows 7:

1 Click **Start**, then click **Control Panel**. In the 'Control Panel' window, click **Hardware and Sound** and then click **Device Manager**.

Jargon buster

Bluetooth A type of short-range wireless connection for transferring data between devices.
Wi-fi A wireless high-speed networking system that can transfer data at high speeds across lots of different devices.

2 In the 'Device Manager' window, click the **small arrow** next to the 'Bluetooth Radios' listing to reveal a list of two Bluetooth device entries. Right click the name of your Bluetooth device (it's the one that's **not** labelled 'Microsoft Bluetooth Enumerator'), and is typically named something like 'Intel Centrino Wireless Bluetooth'.

3 From the menu that appears, click **Disable**. Click **Yes** to the message: 'Disabling this device will cause it to stop functioning. Do you really want to disable it?' Bluetooth will now stop working, and the Bluetooth device icon will feature a down arrow to show it is disabled.

4 To re-enable it at any time, repeat Steps 1-3, but instead of selecting 'Disable' from the menu in Step 3, click **Enable**. Bluetooth will then work as normal.

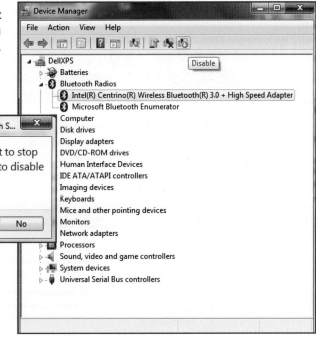

Move to a better power setting

Your laptop should automatically switch to a more conservative power plan whenever your PC is running on battery power, but it's worth checking this.

1 Click **Start**, then click **Control Panel** and then click **Hardware and Sound**.

2 In the new window that appears, click **Power Options**.

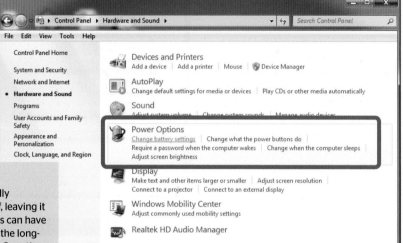

Tip

When your laptop is fully charged and turned off, leaving it plugged-in to the mains can have a debilitating effect on the long-term life of the battery. Over time all batteries lose a portion of their capacity and need to be replaced, but avoiding this mistake will maximise the battery's lifetime.

3 A window will appear titled 'Select a power plan' and listing several power plans. Click the 'Show additional plans' **drop-down arrow**.

4 If the 'High performance' option is selected, then change this to **Balanced**. To extend the battery time even further, you can select **Power saver**. This will give you the maximum time running your laptop from its internal battery, though performance will be slower.

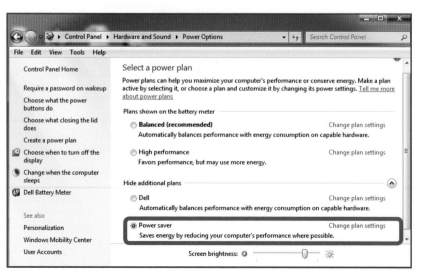

My laptop keeps getting too hot

Today's laptops have speedy processors and powerful components that can quickly get hot. While you're unlikely to burn yourself on a hot laptop, if it overheats it can lead to hardware failure, poor performance and crashes, and ultimately a broken laptop. Here's how to stop your laptop from overheating:

Check your laptop placement

Although the name might suggest that a laptop is ideally located on your lap, this isn't always the best place for keeping it cool. It's important to keep space for air to flow between the bottom of the laptop and where it is sitting. Having a laptop sitting on your lap or a cushion can end up trapping heat, especially since your own lap is naturally warm. Also, cushions can easily wrap around a laptop's ventilation points, increasing the risk of overheating.

Tip
To check the temperature your computer is running at, use a free utility such as HWMonitor. Download it from www.cpuid.com/softwares/hwmonitor.html and install it following the on-screen instructions. Once installed, it displays a window that lists the temperature of your computer's processor and whether the fans are working.

If possible, try to place your laptop on a flat, rigid surface such as a desk or table. If you do want to balance on your lap, balance the laptop on a flat surface, such as a large tray, before placing it on your lap.

Use power management tools

You can take steps to stop your computer from overheating using the power management tools and power saver modes. This can adjust which computer components receive power, such as only those currently being used. If you're suffering from an overly hot laptop, you can adjust the 'Power Settings' in Windows 7 and reduce the power going to the main processor. Try reducing the maximum power going to the processor.

1 Click **Start**, then click **Control Panel**. In the window that appears, click **Hardware and Sound**.

2 In the new window that appears, click **Power Options**. A window will appear titled 'Select a power plan' and listing several power plans. Click the text **Change plan settings** alongside the plan that is currently selected.

Change plan settings

3 At the bottom of the new window that appears, click **Change advanced power settings**.

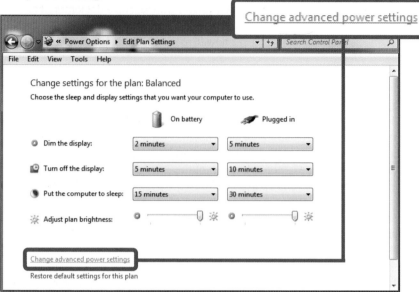

4 From the 'Power Options' window you can manage the power settings of each component in your computer, such as the graphics card and even USB ports.

5 Click the **+** next to 'Processor power management' to expand its options, then click the **+** next to 'Maximum processor state'. Click on the **percentage figure** next to either 'On battery' or 'Plugged in'. Using the small arrows next to the percentage figure, or by typing the figure directly into the percentage box, enter a lower percentage figure such as 80%. This will reduce the speed of your computer slightly, but it will also reduce its temperature. Try adjusting settings on other components as you need to.

If you get in a muddle with adjusting the settings in the 'Power Options' window, you can click **Restore plan defaults** to reset all the changes back to their original settings.

Listen for the fan

A loud whirring noise coming from your laptop is usually an indication that the fan is working hard to keep your computer cool. If the fan noise is very loud, it could mean your computer is too hot. Turn off your computer for 30 minutes to give it time to cool down. If the fan stops making any noise completely, it could be broken and may need to be replaced.

Use a cooling stand

If your laptop is producing a lot of heat, it may be worth considering a cooling stand. These have extra fans that cool the underside of the laptop by circulating air through the insides of your laptop. When choosing a cooling stand, make sure that it fits your laptop snugly and that you buy one suited to your size of laptop. Laptop sizes are usually the size of their screen, such as a 15-inch laptop.

The environment

Keep your laptop in a cool dry place. Water and heat are often the most common causes of damage to laptops. It's also important to keep your laptop environment free of dust. Regularly clean your laptop of dust and grime, especially around the ventilation grilles, which are usually located underneath the laptop, or along the sides. This will make sure that the fans stay clean and that they're able to provide a good flow of air to cool the components.

Prevent Flash from automatically running

Running Adobe Flash in Firefox or Chrome – such as watching online videos or having Flash-powered advertising appear on a web page – can place a huge strain on a laptop's processor. A simple solution is to download Flashblock – an add-on for Firefox that prevents Flash content from automatically running when you load a web page. You can then click on **Flash content** on the web page if you do want to view it. Download it from https://addons.mozilla.org/en-US/firefox/addon/flashblock/.

> ### Jargon buster
> **Adobe Flash** Software that allows your web browser to display video, animation and interactivity on web pages. Commonly used for internet advertising and games.

Internet Explorer has its own built-in Flash blocker of sorts, which will stop Flash from running on a website you visit unless you give Internet Explorer permission.

1 Click **Start**, then click **All Programs** and then click **Internet Explorer** to launch the application.

2 Click the **Tools** menu button in the menu bar above the web page, then click **Manage add-ons**.

3 Click **Toolbars and Extensions** from the left-hand pane, and double click **Shockwave Flash Object**.

Shockwave Flash Object

Manage Add-ons

View and manage your Internet Explorer add-ons

Add-on Types	Name	Publisher	Status	Load time	Navigat
Toolbars and Extensions	(Not verified) Adobe Systems Incorporated.				
Search Providers	Contribute Toolbar	(Not verified) Adobe Sys...	New		
Accelerators	ContributeBHO Class	(Not verified) Adobe Sys...	New		
Tracking Protection	Adobe Systems Incorporated				
	Shockwave Flash Object	Adobe Systems Incorpor...	Enabled		
	Adobe Systems, Incorporated				
	Adobe PDF	Adobe Systems, Incorpo...	New		
Show:	Adobe PDF Link Helper	Adobe Systems, Incorpo...	Enabled	0.10 s	
Currently loaded add-ons	Adobe PDF Conversion Toolbar...	Adobe Systems, Incorpo...	New		

Shockwave Flash Object
Adobe Systems Incorporated

Version: 11.3.300.265
File date:
More information

Type: ActiveX Control
Search for this add-on via default search provider

Disable

Find more toolbars and extensions...
Learn more about toolbars and extensions

Close

More Information

Name:	Shockwave Flash Object
Publisher:	Adobe Systems Incorporated
Type:	ActiveX Control
Status:	Enabled
Version:	11.3.300.265

File date:	
Date last accessed:	13 July 2012, 13:17
Class ID:	{D27CDB6E-AE6D-11CF-96B8-444553540000}
Use count:	4
Block count:	0
File:	Flash32_11_3_300_265.ocx
Folder:	C:\Windows\SysWOW64\Macromed\Flash

Copy

You have approved this add-on to run on the following websites:

*

Remove all sites | Allow on all sites

'Remove all sites' will remove the add-on from all websites. 'Allow on all sites' will allow the control to run on all websites.

Remove | Close

4 In the 'More Information' window that appears, click on the **Remove all sites** button. Close all the open windows. From now on, when you visit a website that has Flash on it, you will get a yellow notification banner asking if you want to display the Flash content, rather than have it load automatically.

Problems with devices

Many PC issues aren't caused by software glitches, but by problematic devices that are connected to your PC. Some devices are obvious – such as a printer or digital camera – and often unplugging them will result in the problem disappearing. But other devices are integral to the PC, such as your computer's graphics card or modem. Windows' Device Manager lets you see which device is causing the problem and offers fixes to help solve the issue.

I've plugged in an external hard drive but it's not showing up

If your hard drive doesn't show up, it could be that Windows 7 can't recognise it. Windows 7 has two features that allow you to manage the devices attached to your PC: Device Manager and Hardware and Sound (see below and overleaf).

Manage your devices in Windows

You can open Device Manager in two ways:

1 Click **Start**, then click **Control Panel**. In the 'Control Panel' window, click **System and Security**. In the window that appears, click on **Device Manager** located under the 'System' section to launch it.

2 Alternatively, click **Start**, then click **Control Panel**. In the 'Control Panel' window, click **Hardware and Sound**. In the window that appears, 'Device Manager' is located under the **Devices and Printers** section. Click **Device Manager** to launch it. The 'Device Manager' window will open.

Check devices are working properly

1 Click the **arrow** or **little triangle** next to each device category to reveal individual hardware components, such as batteries, modems and network adapters.

2 Double click on one of these to reveal a 'Properties' window.

3 If everything is running OK, you will see the message 'This device is working properly' under the 'Device status'.

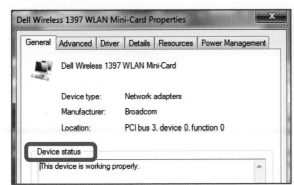

Identify and fix problematic hardware

Problem hardware appears in 'Device Manager' with a small warning icon. A down-pointing arrow symbolises that a device has been disabled.

1 Double click the device and then click **Enable Device** to correct this. If there's a yellow exclamation mark next to a device or it is listed as 'Unknown Device', this usually means that the device driver hasn't installed correctly.

2 Double click the device, click on **Reinstall Driver** and then follow the on-screen instructions.

Use Hardware and Sound

Another tool you can use in Windows to control your computer's internal and external devices is 'Hardware and Sound', located in the 'Control Panel'. Here you can manage your audio, media, printers and so forth.

1 Click **Start**, then click **Control Panel**. In the 'Control Panel' window, click **Hardware and Sound**.

One of the most common problems is when devices don't work or perform as you expect when you connect them, such as a music CD doesn't play or a digital camera doesn't export its images to the computer. The 'Hardware and Sound Control Panel' can solve this using AutoPlay.

1 Click on the **AutoPlay** link in 'Hardware and Sound'.

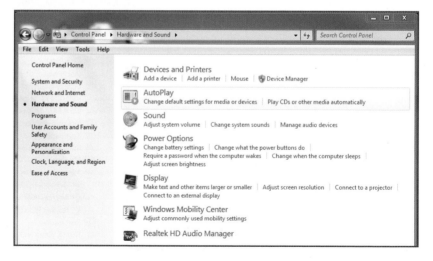

2 Make sure there's a tick in the box next to where it says 'Use AutoPlay for all media and devices'.

3 Click the **down arrow** next to an event and then select the desired outcome. For example, under 'Audio CD' you could choose 'Play audio CD using iTunes'.

4 If you're unsure, select **Ask me every time** and an 'AutoPlay' window will appear every time you insert the media or device, allowing you to choose an action from the list. Click **Save**.

My keyboard is really slow to show keystrokes

If your keyboard responds too slowly, or even too quickly, it can turn the simplest of typing tasks into a misery. Fortunately, it's easy to adjust the response speed of your keyboard.

When you're tapping away at a keyboard you'd hope to see the words on your screen appearing at a steady speed. But it's not uncommon for keyboard response times to lag behind the typing skills of faster writers, or to outpace those needing more time to adjust to learning a new keyboard.

1 Click **Start**, then click **Control Panel**. In the 'Control Panel' window that appears, click **Ease of Access**.

2 In the 'Ease of Access' window and in the 'Ease of Access Center', click **Change how your keyboard works**. Scroll to the bottom of the window that appears and click on the **Keyboard settings** text link.

Keyboard settings

3 Here you can adjust settings for 'Repeat delay' and 'Repeat rate'. If your keyboard is too slow, **move the slider** for 'Repeat delay' towards 'Long', and **move the slider** for 'Repeat rate' towards 'Slow'. If your keyboard is too quick, **move the slider** for 'Repeat delay' towards 'Short', and **move the slider** for 'Repeat rate' towards 'Fast'.

4 In the text box below the settings, you can press and hold letter keys on the keyboard to test how the sliders affect the keyboard. Once done, click **Apply**, then click **OK**.

Printer problems

Is your printer churning out gobbledegook? Got a printer error or problem you can't fix? Printing problems can be some of the most frustrating of all computing challenges. Even worse, printing problems can be costly – wasting ink and paper on printouts that are then tossed into the recycling bin. Here are some common printing problems – and the steps to take to fix them.

When I print a photo, the colours seem wrong or faded

It's likely that your ink cartridges are running low or the ink nozzles are clogged. Depending on your printer brand, you can use the included software you installed when you set up your PC to check the ink levels of your printer. To do this, click **Start**, then click **All Programs** and locate the folder with the name of your printer. Click the folder and locate a utility program for the printer. Double click it to run, and use it to display the current ink levels.

You can also print a test page to check if any of the ink nozzles are blocked.

1 To print a test page, click **Start**, then click **Devices and Printers**.

2 Right click on the icon of the printer you're using, then select **Printer Properties**.

3 On the **General** tab, click on the **Print Test Page** button.

The test page will show samples of the individual coloured ink you have installed – typically cyan, yellow and magenta. If one of these is missing or faded, switch off the printer at the power source, then switch it back on again so that it resets and self-cleans. Repeat steps 1 and 2 above to print a new test page. If you still have problems, you may need to replace your old printer cartridge.

Text appears upside down when I try to print on both sides of the paper

How your printer handles duplex – or double-sided – printing will vary, and if it doesn't automate it in the printer (most don't), it's vital that you follow any on-screen instructions and know which way to stack the paper.

Once you have printed the first side of the paper sheet, you will need to reinsert the paper back into the printer. Look for a helpful guide symbol inscribed on the paper tray, and you can use this to work out whether the printer prints on the side facing up in the paper tray or the side facing down, and whether it prints top to bottom or bottom to top.

If simply flipping the sheet over doesn't work, try flipping it and turning it around in the tray to get double-sided copies.

When I print a document, some of my text or image ends up off the side of the page

If text is being cropped or chopped off the edges of a page, this is typically because the incorrect paper size has been set as the default. You need to check the paper size when printing a document to make sure it matches the paper you have placed in the printer. The steps you take to do this will vary by application. Here's how to check in Word:

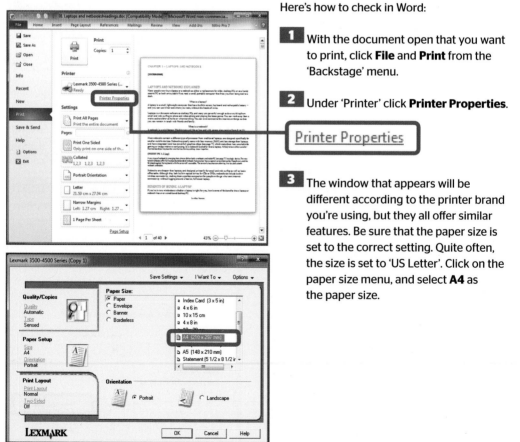

1 With the document open that you want to print, click **File** and **Print** from the 'Backstage' menu.

2 Under 'Printer' click **Printer Properties**.

3 The window that appears will be different according to the printer brand you're using, but they all offer similar features. Be sure that the paper size is set to the correct setting. Quite often, the size is set to 'US Letter'. Click on the paper size menu, and select **A4** as the paper size.

4 Click the various tabs in the 'Printer Properties' window and check for two options: 'Borderless Printing' and 'Borderless Auto Fit'. Check these are turned on by placing a tick next to them. This will ensure that nothing is cropped off by the margins.

5 Click **OK** to close the 'Properties' window. Finally, look for an option in the main 'Print' window under 'Settings' called 'Scale to Paper Size'. Set this to **A4**, and everything you want should come out on the finished page. Click **Print** to print the document.

When I print labels they don't print properly

Printing labels can be a tricky business, but there's a fix to ensure that your labels are perfectly aligned when printing. By downloading templates for applications such as Word, you can then easily use industry-standard labels made by companies such as Avery.

1 Enter www.avery. co.uk into the address bar of the web browser. In the left-hand panel, click **Find a Template**.

2 On the page that appears, click **Blank Templates** on the left-hand column. From here you can choose the template you need by clicking its name, then clicking **Download Template** in the page that appears.

3 Once downloaded, open the template in the software you're using – such as Microsoft Word – and enter the information. Once done, you should be able to print onto the Avery labels inserted into your printer.

My printer is printing gibberish and spits out paper

This could be a driver issue, meaning you need to reload or update the software that runs your printer.

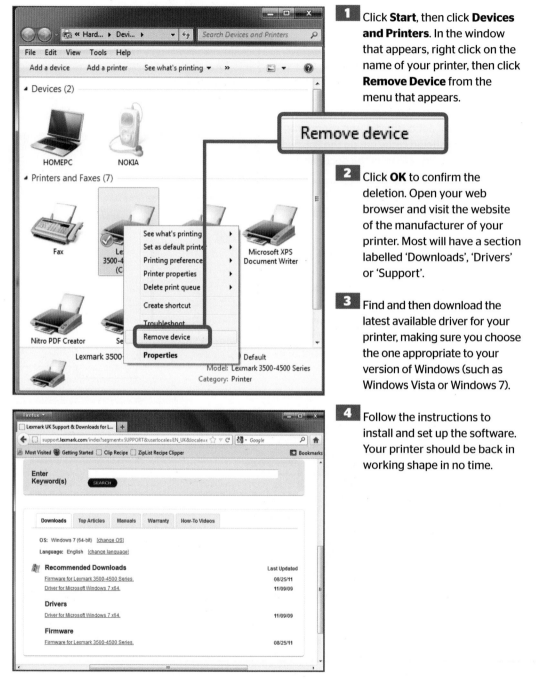

1 Click **Start**, then click **Devices and Printers**. In the window that appears, right click on the name of your printer, then click **Remove Device** from the menu that appears.

2 Click **OK** to confirm the deletion. Open your web browser and visit the website of the manufacturer of your printer. Most will have a section labelled 'Downloads', 'Drivers' or 'Support'.

3 Find and then download the latest available driver for your printer, making sure you choose the one appropriate to your version of Windows (such as Windows Vista or Windows 7).

4 Follow the instructions to install and set up the software. Your printer should be back in working shape in no time.

Whenever I print a document, I get a weird effect where my text or images are ghosted by a tiny area of colour to one side

It sounds like the ink nozzles in your printer are misaligned, meaning that the colours don't mix properly when the ink is added to the paper. Each printer has its own alignment routine, which is usually detailed in the printer's manual. In some cases you will find it as an option in the driver:

1 Click **Start**, then click **Devices and Printers**. In the window that appears, locate your printer and right click it and select **Printer properties**.

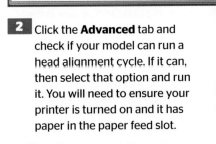

2 Click the **Advanced** tab and check if your model can run a head alignment cycle. If it can, then select that option and run it. You will need to ensure your printer is turned on and it has paper in the paper feed slot.

3 Alternatively, many printers include their own troubleshooting software that is installed when you first set up your printer. Click on the **Start** button, then click **All Programs** and locate the folder of applications for your printer. Look for a troubleshooting program (in this example, the Lexmark Solutions Center tool has been used) and launch it. Look for tools for fixing alignment problems.

Some all-in-one scanner/printers have an auto-alignment feature, where you print a sheet then scan it in. Again, check your manual for details.

My document won't print because another document is clogging up the print queue

Your printer software organises jobs into a queue and if one job fails this can prevent any other work from being done. The only symptom can be that files you send to the printer simply stop being printed out.

1 To check if there is a document holding up the print queue, click **Start** and then click **Devices and Printers**.

2 In the window that appears, locate your printer from the list and double click on the icon representing your printer.

3 The status column will display a list of the jobs still waiting to be printed. If one has failed, it will be flagged in the status column together with a reason for the failure.

Lexmark 3500-4500 Series (Copy 1)							
Printer	Document	View					
Docum	Pause		Owner	Pages	Size	Submitted	Port
web	Resume		Eleanor	1	1.86 MB	11:20:04 17/07/2012	
Trair	Restart		Eleanor	1	1.29 MB/1.29 ...	11:17:56 17/07/2012	3500-4
	Cancel						
Cancels t	Properties						

4 To unclog the queue, you need to delete the failed job from the queue. Click on the failed print job, then select **Document** and then **Cancel** from the top menu. Confirm the cancellation, then close the printer's window and restart your computer. When it restarts, the outstanding jobs in the queue should now print.

When I try to print web pages some of the pages are missing?

The good news is that the problem is more likely to be an issue with your web browser or the website, rather than your printer, but you can perform a few checks that might help you print successfully.

1 With the web page open that you want to print, check to see if the page you are looking at has a 'Print' option on it or a 'printer-friendly version'. It can also look like a small printer icon on the web page. Click this and you should see a version of the web page specifically formatted for printing.

2 If the page doesn't have a printer-friendly version, then try adjusting the print settings. From the top menu in your web browser, select **File** and then select **Print Preview** from the menu. In this example, Firefox is used.

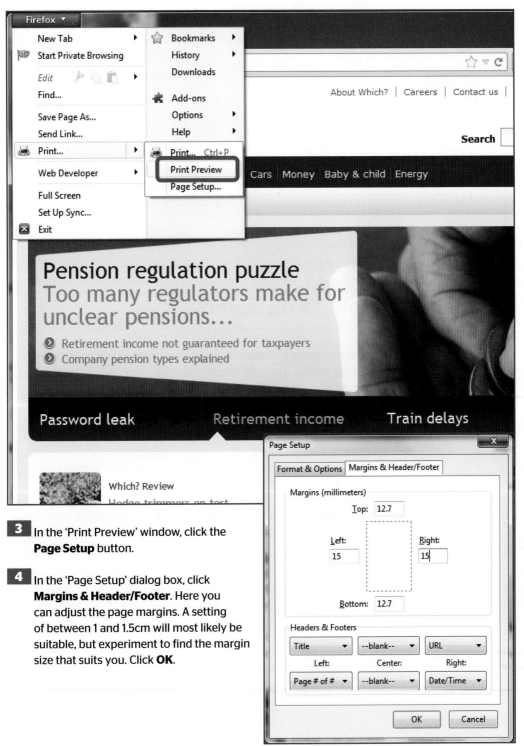

3 In the 'Print Preview' window, click the **Page Setup** button.

4 In the 'Page Setup' dialog box, click **Margins & Header/Footer**. Here you can adjust the page margins. A setting of between 1 and 1.5cm will most likely be suitable, but experiment to find the margin size that suits you. Click **OK**.

5 Back in the 'Print Preview' window, you can also try changing the page orientation setting from its current setting (such as from landscape to portrait, or from portrait to landscape).

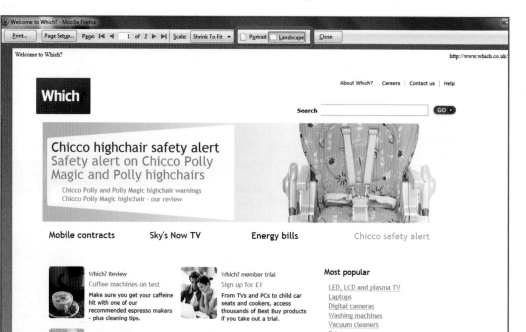

I've replaced my ink cartridge but my printer isn't working

Check you have removed any protective tape or film from the ink cartridge when you put it in. Ink nozzles are usually protected by a translucent strip of tape and you need to remove this before installing the cartridge.

Also try switching the printer on and off at the power source and disconnecting, then reconnecting the USB lead; your computer might not have registered that a new ink cartridge has been fitted. See, too, if there are any indicators flashing on your printer and check in your manual for diagnostic help.

Finally, after installing a new ink cartridge, you may need to press a button to get the printer online and back in action. Refer to the manufacturer's manual.

Email and communication

By reading this chapter you'll get to grips with:

- Fixing email sending and receiving problems
- Making video calls and instant messaging
- Solving Facebook and Twitter account issues

General webmail problems

Traditionally, most email has been sent to software that lives on your PC. The problem is that you need to be at your PC if you want to send, receive and read emails sent to you. You can check and go through your emails, write new messages and replies even when you're not online, but to send and receive emails you need to be connected to the internet. The answer is to move to a free webmail account such as Gmail, Yahoo! Mail or Windows Live Mail.

Webmail accounts can only be accessed when you're connected to the internet, but the benefit is that you can access your email easily from any computer or device, not just your home computer. The most well-known accounts are Gmail, Yahoo! Mail, AOL Mail and Windows Live Hotmail.

Many email clients now allow you to add your webmail accounts so you can read all your email in one place.

However, webmail – while handy – can have its own set of problems ...

When I try to access my webmail, Internet Explorer doesn't respond

The wrong date and time settings on your PC can cause your web browser to hang or even crash when trying to access web-based email servers. If this happens, check your PC's date and time settings.

1 Click **Start**, then click **Control Panel**.

2 Click **Clock, Language, and Region**.

3 Click **Date and Time**.

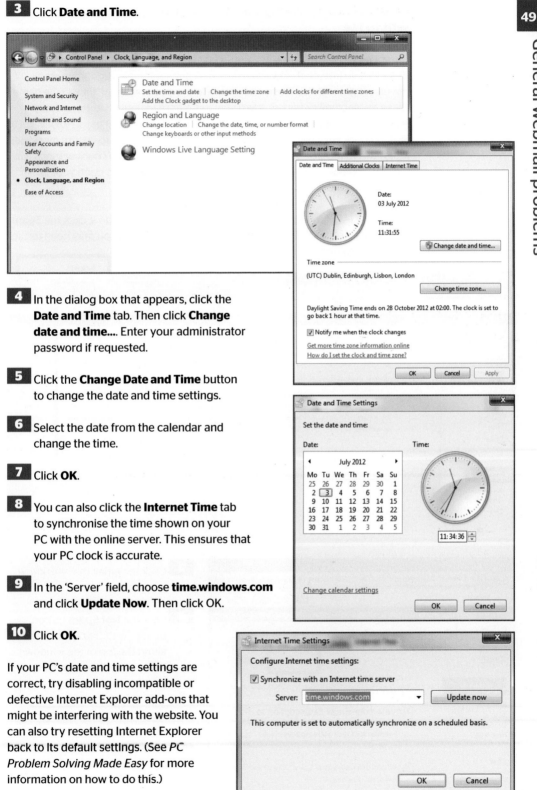

4 In the dialog box that appears, click the **Date and Time** tab. Then click **Change date and time...**. Enter your administrator password if requested.

5 Click the **Change Date and Time** button to change the date and time settings.

6 Select the date from the calendar and change the time.

7 Click **OK**.

8 You can also click the **Internet Time** tab to synchronise the time shown on your PC with the online server. This ensures that your PC clock is accurate.

9 In the 'Server' field, choose **time.windows.com** and click **Update Now**. Then click OK.

10 Click **OK**.

If your PC's date and time settings are correct, try disabling incompatible or defective Internet Explorer add-ons that might be interfering with the website. You can also try resetting Internet Explorer back to its default settings. (See *PC Problem Solving Made Easy* for more information on how to do this.)

Help! I'm not receiving emails that I know have been sent to me

After you have checked that the person sending emails to you is using the correct email address, look in your Spam folder. Webmail providers use spam filters to help intercept unwanted junk mail but sometimes legitimate email can be caught in these filters and placed in the 'junk' or 'spam' folder (the name varies by webmail provider). It will stay there unread until it's automatically deleted – this happens after a set number of days, usually 30 days. However, it's best to check your webmail provider's Spam folder settings to ensure messages within this folder are not being deleted immediately. How to check settings will vary by webmail provider – in this example, Gmail is used. To open your Spam folder, follow these steps:

1 In the list of folders on the left side of the webmail window, click the **Spam** folder to open it. Depending on the specific webmail, you may need to click **More** to expand the list to show the Spam folder.

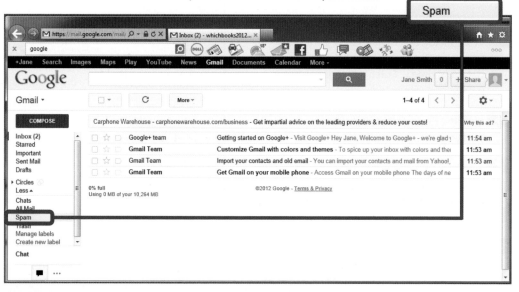

2 Click the email that you know is not spam.

3 Click the **Not Spam** button, or your webmail's equivalent, along the top of the window. The email will be moved to your Inbox.

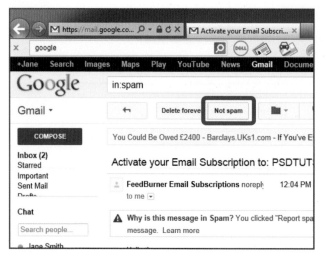

Marking an email as not spam makes it less likely that email from this sender will be marked as spam in the future. However, you can increase the chance of this happening by taking the following steps:

■ Add senders to your contact list or email address book. Spam filters often look here to decide if a message is spam. If the sender is listed in your address book, then the email is less likely to be considered spam.

■ If your webmail allows, add the sender to a whitelist, or set up a rule or filter (see pages 58-9) so that messages from this sender are never marked as spam.

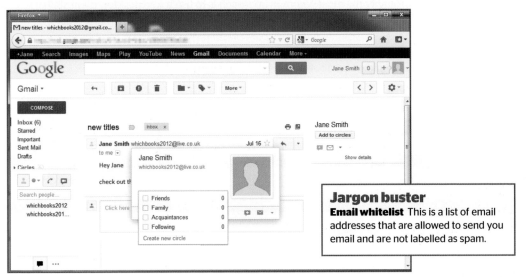

Jargon buster
Email whitelist This is a list of email addresses that are allowed to send you email and are not labelled as spam.

I'm receiving bounce back messages from emails that I haven't sent

Your webmail address has been spoofed. Spammers often forge the 'From' sender on the spam or phishing emails they send, making it look as if the message came from someone else. It means that when the email is rejected by the recipient's mail server, the bounce back message goes to whoever is named in the outgoing mail rather than to the spammer themselves.

At present, there's little you can do to avoid this nuisance - short of obtaining a new webmail address. If you don't want to do this, delete the bounce back messages. You can create a rule or filter (see pages 58-9) for your Inbox to delete the unwanted messages automatically. You will probably find that after a short while they'll stop arriving completely. This is because other webmail servers will have designated the message as spam.

The good news is that being spoofed doesn't mean your account has been accessed. However, ensure your webmail security settings are in place and change your password. See page 105 for tips in creating a strong password.

My webmail provider has lost all my webmail

No matter how great many webmail services are, they're not infallible when it comes to storing your data. So it's sensible to back up your email just in case things go amiss. To accomplish this, you can use a standalone backup program such as Gmail Backup or a third-party web service such as Backupify, but probably the most common approach is to use a free desktop client such as Windows Live Mail, Apple Mail, Mozilla Thunderbird and many others.

You will need to change your webmail settings from IMAP to POP. So, for example, in Gmail after you have signed in:

1 Click the **Settings** icon (it looks like a gear cog in the upper-right corner).

2 From the drop-down menu click **Settings**.

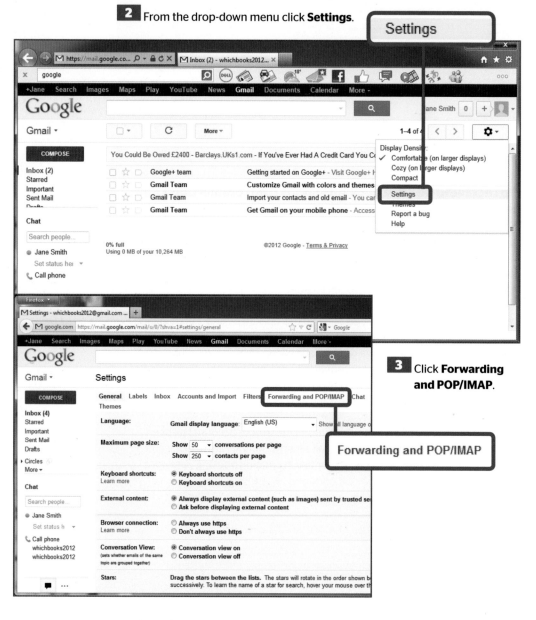

3 Click **Forwarding and POP/IMAP**.

4 Under 'POP Download' point 1, select 'Enable POP1 for all mail (even mail that's already been downloaded)'.

53

General webmail problems

5 Under 'POP Download' point 2, click the 'When messages are accessed with POP' **drop-down arrow** and select **Keep Gmail's copy in the inbox** from the drop-down list.

6 Click **Save Changes**.

7 Then you need to set up your desktop email program (known as an 'email client'). Google for example offers step-by-step instructions for different email clients on its website (http://support.google.com/mail) for a number of programs – just be sure to use POP instead of IMAP for one-way message transfers.

8 When you first enable POP in your Gmail settings, all messages are downloaded to the email client, except for spam, trash and chats. Messages arrive in batches so it can take some time for them all to download if you have lots of messages. New messages will be then downloaded automatically each time you launch the desktop client.

Jargon buster

Email client A program installed on your PC that manages your emails. Emails are stored on your hard drive and you only need to be connected to the internet to send and receive emails.
IMAP: IMAP (Internet message access protocol) lets you download messages from Gmail so you can access your mail with a program like Outlook Express or Apple Mail. IMAP syncs the actions you take in Outlook Express or Apple Mail with Gmail so if you read a message in your mail client, it'll be marked as read in Gmail.
POP (Post office protocol) A way of allowing an email server (a computer dedicated to delivering email) to 'post' emails to your computer.

Windows Live Mail

Windows Live Mail is Microsoft's email program. Hailed as the big brother of Outlook Express and replacing Windows Mail on Windows Vista, Windows Live Mail has a simple interface and useful features. It doesn't come pre-installed on Windows 7 but can be downloaded as part of Windows Live Essentials.

When I print an email from Windows Live Mail, the start of each line is missing

When part of a page or text is chopped off when printing it's usually solved by adjusting page margins within the application, but unfortunately, there's no way to set printer margins in Windows Live Mail. However, there is a way around this problem. Windows Live Mail shares the same print engine as Internet Explorer so you can adjust page margin in the web browser instead. Here's how:

1 Open Internet Explorer.

2 Click the **Tools** icon (it looks like a cog) on the top right of the window. From the drop-down menu point to 'Print' and then click **Page Setup**.

3 In the 'Page Setup' dialog box, adjust the margins to your liking. Setting the page margins to 19.05 mm for top, bottom, left and right should be fine, but you can print a page to test and then readjust if required.

4 Under 'Paper Options' you can change the orientation of your page by choosing Portrait or Landscape. Click **OK**.

I can't see the columns I want in Windows Live Mail

You can select which information is shown in the columns in your Windows Live Mail folders – so, for example, you can choose to show email size as a column. Be aware however, that changing the column layout of one folder automatically changes the layout of all other folders.

1 Click **Start**, then **All Programs**, and then click **Windows Mail** and sign in.

2 Click the **View** tab, and then click **View** and from the drop-down menu click **Select Columns...**.

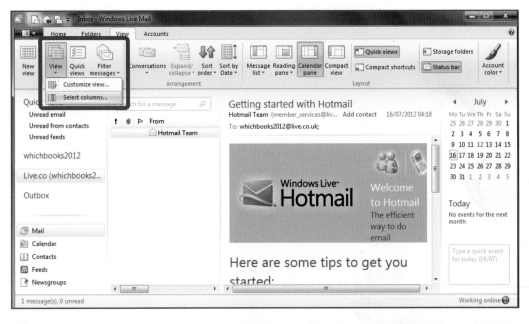

3 To add a column, select the check box next to the column name.

4 To remove a column, clear the check box next to the column name.

5 To change the order in which columns appear, click a column name, and then click **Move Up** or **Move Down**.

Columns

Check the columns that you would like visible in this view. Use the Move Up and Move Down buttons to reorder the columns however you like.

- ☑ Priority
- ☑ Attachment
- ☑ Flag
- ☑ From
- ☑ Subject
- ☑ Date
- ☐ Mark for Offline
- ☐ Size

[Move Up] [Move Down] [Show] [Hide] [Reset]

The selected column should be `75` pixels wide.

[OK] [Cancel]

Help! I can't find all the messages I know I've received on the same subject

You may have lots of email messages on the same topic that are scattered through your Inbox. By grouping related messages, you can keep track of the conversation. You can choose to view only the original message, or the message and all of the replies.

1 In Windows Live Mail, click the **View** tab.

2 In the 'Arrangement' group, click **Conversations** and then click **On** from the drop-down menu.

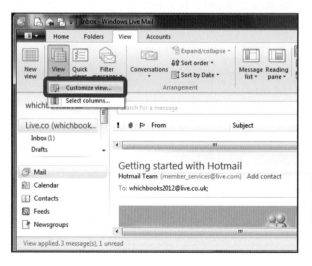

3 To expand a conversation, click the **right-pointing triangle** in front of the oldest message in the thread.

I keep losing sight of all my unread email

Windows Live Mail lets you create a customised view so you can choose which messages are displayed, which can fix this problem. You can, for example, choose to show only messages on a specific subject or unread messages from a particular sender.

1 In Windows Mail, click the **View** tab.

2 Click **View** and from the resulting drop-down menu select **Customize view...**.

3 In the 'Customize Current View' dialog box, select one or more conditions for the view you're creating. As you add conditions, the 'View Description' field changes to show the current list of conditions for your new view.

4 In the 'View Description' field, click an underlined word or phrase to choose an option or enter a value. For example, if you have selected 'Where the Subject line contains specific words' as a condition, click **contains specific words**.

5 In the new dialog box type the words or phrase you want to use and click **Add**, then click **OK**.

6 Type a name for the view, and then click **OK**.

My inbox is swamped with email

To avoid inbox chaos, it's best to organise your email messages and file them into different folders. But there's no need to do this manually as you can use rules in Windows Mail to automatically move messages to the folders that you choose. For example, you may create a rule to move email from a specific person to a folder that has their name attached to it or to delete unwanted messages automatically.

To create a rule

1 In Windows Live Mail, click on the **Folders** tab.

2 Click **Message rules**.

3 In the 'New Mail Rule' dialog box, under 'Select one or more conditions', select one or more check boxes to set up the criteria that will be applied to incoming messages.

4 Under 'Select one or more actions', select one or more check boxes to determine how to handle messages that meet the conditions you selected in Step 3.

5 In the description field, click the underlined words or phrases to specify the conditions or actions for your rule.

6 If you have selected more than one condition, click the underlined word 'and' in the description field. Then in the 'And/Or' dialog box, click **Messages match all of the criteria** or **Messages match any one of the criteria**, and then click **OK**.

7 Type a new name that describes your rule, and then click **Save rule** and then click **OK**.

I can't open an email attachment

As a security measure, Windows Live Mail blocks some email attachments that it deems to have a higher risk of containing a virus. If it does, you will see the warning 'Prohibited file type' displayed in the message header and you won't be able to download or open the attachment.

> **BE CAREFUL!**
> As disabling this feature isn't recommended from a security point of view, consider reinstating it for future emails.

If, however, you know the origin of a particular attachment and are happy to open the file, you can disable this setting in Live Mail's Safety options. Once changed, you will then be able to download and open all types of attachments. As altering this setting won't unblock attachments that Live Mail has already received, you may need to ask the sender to resend the email with the attachment.

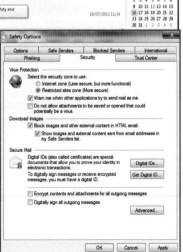

1 In Windows Live Mail, on the **Home** tab, click **Junk** and then click **Safety options...**.

2 On the 'Safety Options' dialog box, click the **Security** tab.

3 Under 'Virus Protection', clear the check box next to 'Do not allow attachments to be saved or opened that could potentially be a virus.'

4 Click **OK**.

Gmail

Google's Gmail is a popular free webmail service that allows you to store email remotely on its servers so you can access it from any computer or internet-enabled device.

I've logged on to Gmail using a friend's computer but I'm missing features

It may be that the web browser you're using isn't fully supported by Gmail. When you sign in to Gmail on an unsupported browser, you will see a basic HTML version with some features missing, such as the spell checker, rich formatting and keyboard shortcuts, as well as the ability to add filters and manage contacts.

Jargon buster

HTML An abbreviation of HyperText Markup Language, the computer programming language that is used to create web pages.

To access all of Gmail's features, use a supported browser that has cookies (small text files that store information about you, such as login details and passwords) and is JavaScript enabled. Gmail supports most versions of the popular web browsers, but you can check your browser version at http://support.google.com/mail/bin/answer. py?hl=en&answer=6557. If, after changing your browser, the problem persists, disable any browser extensions or add-ons to see if they're causing Gmail to default to the basic HTML version. (See *PC Problem Solving Made Easy* for more information on how to do this.)

I'm getting the error message 'In order to log in to Gmail, your browser must be set to allow JavaScript to set cookies'

Gmail needs cookies to be enabled in your browser in order to work properly. You need to enable cookies by changing your browser's preferences or options and if you have a third-party cookie manager, you need to configure it to allow cookies from Gmail. Here's how to enable cookies for Gmail in Internet Explorer:

1 Open Internet Explorer and click the **Tools** icon (it looks like a cog) on the top right of the window. Click on **Internet options** on the drop-down menu.

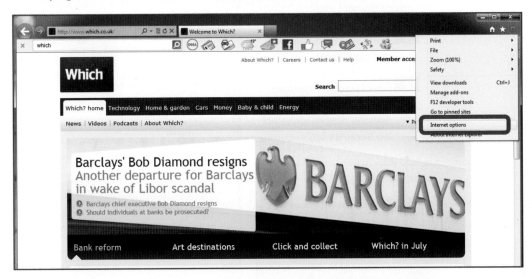

2 In the 'Internet Options' dialog box, click the **Privacy** tab, and then **move the slider** halfway between the top and bottom so you're not blocking or allowing ALL cookies. Click **Sites**.

3 In the 'Address of website' box, enter the following sites and click **Allow** for each:
https://www.google.com
https://mail.google.com
http://b.mail.google.com.
Then click **OK**.

4 Move the slider back to the position it was originally in, and then click **OK** to save your changes.

It's also a good idea to add Gmail to the list of trusted sites within Internet Explorer:

1 Open Internet Explorer and click **Tools**.

2 Select **Internet Options** and then in the 'Internet Options' dialog box select the **Security** tab.

3 Click **Trusted sites** and then **Sites**.

4 Enter https://www.google.com in the 'Add this Website to the zone' field and click **Add**.

5 Enter https://gmail.google.com and click **Add**.

6 Click **OK** to save your changes.

I can't access my Gmail account on my iPhone any more

If you have been able to access your Gmail account through a device such as a mobile phone or through a desktop email client such as Outlook, but now you can't, it may be as a result of turning on Gmail's 2-step verification.

Gmail's 2-step verification process doesn't work with all applications, however. You need to create an application specific password (to be used in place of your regular password) for any client/application/device, including your iPhone, that doesn't support the 2-step code. Alternatively, you can disable the 2-step verification feature.

Generate an application-specific password

1 Log on to your account and click the **drop-down arrow** next to your profile picture or your account name (usually your Gmail address) in the upper-right area of the screen.

2 Click **Account**, then click **Security**. In the page that appears click **Edit** next to 'Authorizing applications and sites'.

3 You may need to re-enter your password at this point – do so, and click **Verify**.

4 Under the 'Application-specific passwords' section, enter a descriptive name for the application you want to authorise, such as 'iPhone', then click **Generate password**.

5 The application-specific password will be displayed along with the name you gave for the application. You also have the option here to revoke (cancel) the code or codes you have previously generated.

6 Make a note of the password as once you have clicked **Done**, you will be unable to view that application-specific code again. However, you can always generate a new one – even for devices or applications that you have authorised before.

Use an application-specific password

When signing in to your Gmail account on a non-browser application or device:

1 Enter your username.

2 Enter your application-specific password in the password field.

3 If your application has an option to remember the password or stay signed in, you can select this and then you won't have to generate and enter a new password each time you access your account from this application or device.

Turn off 2-step verification

1 Log on to your account and click **Accounts**.

2 Click **Security** and then next to '2-step verification', click **Edit**.

3 Click **Turn off 2-step verification**.

4 A pop-up window will appear to confirm that you want to turn off 2-step verification. Click **OK**.

I want to send mail from linked Gmail accounts

Many people have more than one Gmail address that they use for different purposes. You may use one for work, one for personal, one for registering on new websites you're not totally sure of and so forth. Previously, Gmail allowed you to access only one account at a time per browser. Now, however you can link multiple accounts and view them in the same account window.

Once accounts are linked, you can then choose which address to send an email from – all within the same account window and browser tab. To do this, follow these steps:

1 Click the **Settings** icon (it looks like a gear cog) at the top right of the page.

2 From the drop-down menu click **Settings**.

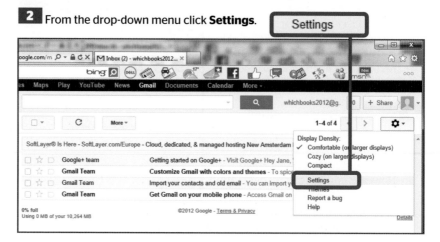

3 Click **Accounts and Import**, then next to 'Send mail as' click **Add another email address you own**.

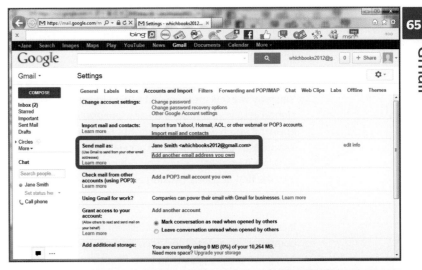

4 In the window that appears, enter your name and the email address that you want to use and click **Next Step**.

Gmail will need to verify this by sending an email. Follow the instructions to verify you have this account.

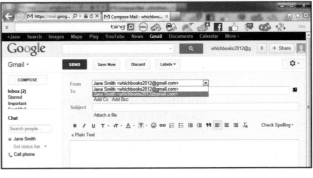

5 Once verified, when you select **Compose** to create a new message, you will have the option to select which email address to use.

I think someone has accessed my account – how can I be sure?

If you're concerned about unauthorised access to your account, you can use Gmail's 'Last account activity information' to check. This shows details about the most recent activity in your Gmail account including when the account was accessed through a web browser, a POP1 client, a mobile device and so on. It also lists all the IP addresses that accessed your mail, the associated location, plus the time and date.

1 To access this information, click the **Details** link next to the 'Last account activity' line at the bottom of any Gmail page.

2 Look at the 'Access Type' column to find out if someone has accessed your mail. For example, if the column shows any POP access, but you don't use POP to collect your mail, it may be a sign that your account has been compromised.

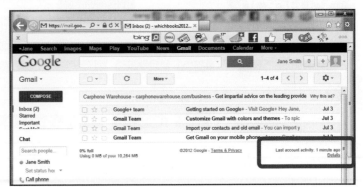

Yahoo! Mail

Yahoo! Mail is a free email service that is offered by the US search engine company Yahoo!

I get the message, 'Your login session has expired'

You may see this message if it's been more than eight hours since you last signed in to your Yahoo! Mail account and still haven't signed out. Or it may appear if you have opened another browser window and logged into a second Yahoo! Mail account. You can access only one Yahoo! Mail account at a time so this automatically signs you out of the first account. When you log back into the first account, clicking any link gives you the 'your login session has expired' message.

It is a security measure, especially for those who use public or shared computers to access their accounts, so if you see the message you will have to log in again by providing your username and password.

If you see this message more often, check that the time on your PC is accurate. Incorrect time settings on your computer can result in web browsers having difficulty managing cookie files (see page 60) and therefore may generate error messages more frequently.

My messages are being incorrectly labelled as spam but the Spam folder is empty

If this happens, check your Spam folder settings. It's likely that they've been set to delete spam immediately, so you will need to change this:

1 Click **Options** on the navigation bar at the top of the page, then click **Mail Options** from the drop-down menu.

2 The general Mail options should open by default. If not, click **General** in the left-hand pane.

3 Under 'Spam Protection', make sure the check box for **Automatically move spam to Spam folder** is ticked if you want messages identified as spam to be saved in the Spam folder. If it's unticked, spam will be deleted immediately.

4 Click the 'Empty Spam folder' field **drop-down arrow** and select either **Once a week**, **Every two weeks** or **Once a month**.

5 Click the yellow **Save Changes** button at the top-right of the screen.

I'm not receiving emails

If you're missing emails that you know have been sent, there are a number of things that might have happened.

The email was not addressed properly

The sender may have the wrong address or made a mistake typing it. The incorrectly spelt address for you may actually be someone else's email address. If so, they'll receive the email, and the sender won't be aware of their mistake.

The email was delayed

Email delivery normally takes just a few minutes, but sometimes delivery can be delayed because of heavy internet traffic or mail server problems.

The sender's address is blocked

Yahoo! Mail lets you block addresses that you don't want to receive mail from. If an email is sent from one of these addresses, Yahoo! Mail will discard it. To check your blocked addresses list:

 Click **Options** on the navigation bar at the top of the page, then click **Mail Options** from the drop-down menu.

2 Click **Blocked Addresses** on the left and blocked addresses will be listed to the right.

You have set up mail forwarding

Check to see if your mail is being forwarded to another email address:

1 Click **Options** on the navigation bar at the top of the page, then click **Mail Options** from the drop-down menu.

2 Click **POP & Forwarding** on the left.

3 If, next to 'Forward Yahoo! Mail to another email address', there is a dot, then you are forwarding emails to a different address. To disable this, click to remove the dot.

You have created filters

You may have set up a filter that means your email is being sent to the Trash folder or to another folder within your Yahoo! Mail account. To check:

1 Click **Options** on the navigation bar at the top of the page, then click **Mail Options** from the drop-down menu.

2 Click **Filters**. If filters are listed, check that they're not set to prevent receiving emails from this sender.

The email may have been mistaken as spam

Check your Spam folder for the missing email, and also check your Spam folder settings to make sure messages are not being deleted immediately. To check your Spam folder settings see pages 66–7.

No matter what the reason, the best solution is to ask the sender to re-send the email. It's also a good idea to add the sender's email address to your Contacts list, so they're recognised as legitimate senders and not spam.

Help, I've deleted an email by mistake

When you delete email messages from your Inbox or other folders, they're moved into the Trash folder. As long as the Trash folder hasn't been emptied or the folder settings aren't set to delete immediately, you can retrieve a deleted message from your Trash folder by moving the message from Trash to another folder. However, Yahoo! Mail can permanently remove the messages in your Trash folder at any time without warning, so it's best not to put emails in the trash if you may want them later.

I can't send an email

If you can't send, reply or forward email, it may be because something installed on your computer is preventing the Yahoo! Mail 'Color and Graphics' toolbar from fully launching.

As a way around this, try switching to plain text.

1 Click **Compose Message** and then under the Subject line to the right, click **Switch to Plain Text**.

2 You can switch back to rich-text formatting by clicking the **Switch to Rich Text** link in the same spot.

Using a webcam

A webcam is a small video camera used for accessing live images through the internet. Mainly used for chatting to friends and family or for business video-calls, A webcam also lets you capture photos and video and stream them across the internet.

Many laptops come with a built-in webcam – usually positioned above the screen and facing you as you look at the screen. You can also plug in an external webcam using a USB cable into a desktop PC.

My computer doesn't recognise my external webcam

The first step is to check that your webcam is properly connected. Most webcams use the USB port to connect to a PC, so check the cable is fully plugged in. Next open Windows 'Device Manager' to see if the hardware is recognised and installed properly:

1 Click **Start**, then click **Control Panel**.

2 In the 'Control Panel' window, click **System and Security**. Under 'System', click **Device Manager**. You may have to enter your administrator password at this point.

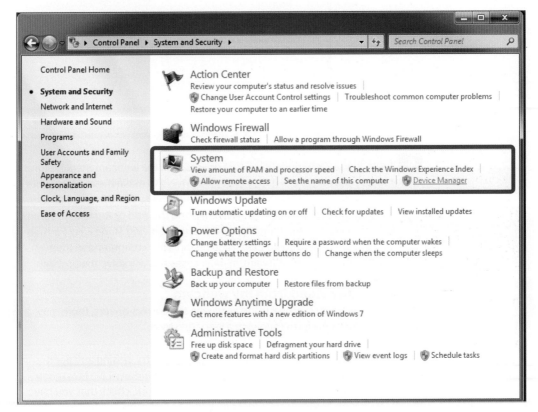

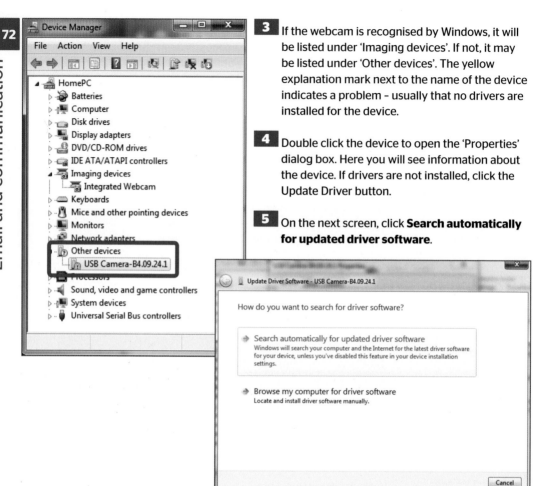

3 If the webcam is recognised by Windows, it will be listed under 'Imaging devices'. If not, it may be listed under 'Other devices'. The yellow explanation mark next to the name of the device indicates a problem – usually that no drivers are installed for the device.

4 Double click the device to open the 'Properties' dialog box. Here you will see information about the device. If drivers are not installed, click the Update Driver button.

5 On the next screen, click **Search automatically for updated driver software**.

6 If Windows fails to find the correct drivers, visit the webcam manufacturer's support site and check if they provided drivers to make the model of your webcam compatible with Windows 7. Alternatively, you can uninstall the software that came with your webcam using the 'Add or Remove Programs' feature in the 'Control Panel' (see *PC Problem Solving Made Easy* for more information on how to do this). Then restart your computer and then reinstall the webcam software. In most cases this will solve the problem.

I can't see any video from my webcam

Even if your webcam is properly installed with the correct drivers, there may be other reasons why it isn't showing a live video feed.

Another program may be using your webcam, so first try closing any open video-editing software, instant messengers such as Windows Live Messenger, web browsers and Windows Explorer. If this doesn't work, check that you have the latest version of Microsoft DirectX installed as webcams use this for video processing. The way to check this is described opposite.

1 Click **Start** and type **run** in the search box. Double click on the **Run** icon at the top of the window.

2 In the 'Run' dialog box type **dxdiag** and click **OK**. The 'DirectX Diagnostic Tool' dialog box opens.

Programs (1)
- Run

Control Panel (10)
- Run programs made for previous versions of Windows
- View recommended actions to keep Windows running smoothly
- Show which operating system your computer is running
- View running processes with Task Manager

Documents (36)
- Running
- Script for history project
- smoking-RE

Eleanor (61)
- p14 - I'm not sure my computer can run Windows 7 - step 1
- p14 - I'm not sure my computer can run Windows 7 - step 2
- p14 - I'm not sure my computer can run Windows 7 - step 2

Pictures (11)
- p14 - I'm not sure my computer can run Windows 7 - step 2
- p14 - I'm not sure my computer can run Windows 7 - step 1
- p24 - What programs are running at startup - step 1

See more results

run   ×   Shut down ▶

Run

Type the name of a program, folder, document, or Internet resource, and Windows will open it for you.

Open: dxdiag

OK   Cancel   Browse...

3 Click the **System** tab. At the bottom of the 'System Information' section, you will see which version of Direct X is installed.

DirectX Diagnostic Tool

System | Display | Sound | Input

This tool reports detailed information about the DirectX components and drivers installed on your system.

If you know what area is causing the problem, click the appropriate tab above. Otherwise, you can use the "Next Page" button below to visit each page in sequence.

System Information

Current Date/Time: 24 May 2012, 12:43:02
Computer Name: HOMEPC
Operating System: Windows 7 Home Premium 64-bit (6.1, Build 7600)
Language: English (Regional Setting: English)
System Manufacturer: Dell Inc.
System Model: Inspiron 1564
BIOS: Ver 1.00 BIOS A01 PARTTBL
Processor: Intel(R) Core(TM) i3 CPU   M 330 @ 2.13GHz (4 CPUs), ~2.1GHz
Memory: 4096MB RAM
Page file: 1900MB used, 5882MB available
DirectX Version: DirectX 11

☑ Check for WHQL digital signatures

DxDiag 6.01.7600.16385 32-bit Unicode Copyright © 1998-2006 Microsoft Corporation. All rights reserved.

Help | Run 64-bit DxDiag | Next Page | Save All Information... | Exit

4 Click **Exit** to close the 'DirectX Diagnostic Tool' window.

5 If necessary, download and install the latest version of DirectX from the Microsoft DirectX site.

The video on my webcam looks terrible

If your webcam's image looks poor quality and blurry, there are a several things that can help. First try lowering your screen resolution. To do this:

1 Right click on your desktop and click **Properties** and then **Screen Resolution**.

2 Reduce screen resolution one level below where it's currently set and test the image quality. If it needs further sharpening, repeat the process until you achieve the desired clarity.

View	▶
Sort by	▶
Refresh	
Paste	
Paste shortcut	
Graphics Properties...	
Graphics Options	▶
New	▶
Screen resolution	
Gadgets	
Personalize	

3 Next optimise the settings used in your video chat program. If you're using Skype, for example, select **Tools** and click on the **Video** icon in the left toolbar. Click **Webcam Settings** and adjust the visual and camera function settings as well as lighting compensation.

4 If you continue to suffer from poor image-quality, check your internet bandwidth settings. To broadcast a good quality video session requires a minimum bandwidth connection of 1Mbps. If network traffic is high, or other users are sharing the same internet connection, it may lower the quality of your video projection. Visit an online test site like www.speedtest.co.uk and run a bandwidth check.

Help! My webcam image looks washed out

Lighting is very important when using a webcam and a common issue involves maintaining a decent image in either very bright or low-light conditions. If you find that your face appears too washed out or is in semi-darkness, here are some ways to improve the lighting.

Tweak webcam settings

Make sure your webcam settings – particularly brightness contrast, hue and saturation – suit the lighting in the room. To access your webcam settings, click **Start** and type **webcam** in the search box. This should show the software for your integrated webcam. Click the name to open the program and click on **Settings** to open the setting controls. Use the sliders to adjust the settings for your web broadcast.

Lights, camera, action!

Don't use your laptop screen as a light source. Turn on a main light or desk light, but don't direct it straight at your face – too much light close to the webcam can blanch the image, making it difficult to see. Aim for diffuse light where possible.

Make sure your desktop image isn't too dark

If your desktop image is dark in colour, swap it for a white background. For example, open a Notepad document and maximise the window so that it covers your desktop. Then increase the brightness on your monitor. The white light will be reflected back onto your face.

All white

To help improve a webcam broadcast, try wearing a white shirt. This will help your webcam's auto white balance/auto-exposure achieve a good white balance and colour exposure.

Location

These lenses are not as good quality as those on camcorders so position yourself fairly close and directly in front of the webcam lens. Also keep the background simple and avoid distracting patterns or movements. If you plan to use your webcam a lot, consider buying a collapsible background disc from Amazon or a photographic supplier.

I don't want my children to use the webcam

There may be reasons why you'd want to turn off your computer's integrated webcam. If you're a parent for example, preventing your children's access to video instant messaging and chat websites may be a priority. Here's how to disable your webcam in Windows 7:

1 Click **Start**, then click **Control Panel** and click on **Hardware and Sound**.

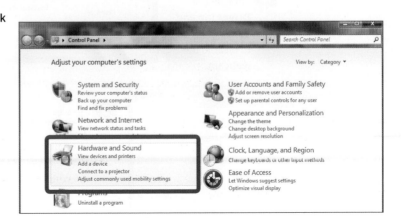

2 Under 'Devices and Printers', click on **Device Manager**.

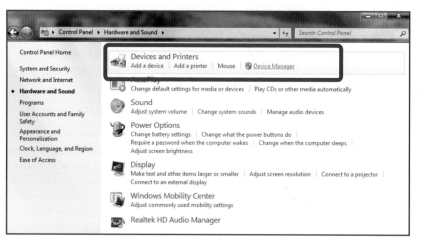

3 Double click on **Imaging devices** and select your webcam by double clicking on it.

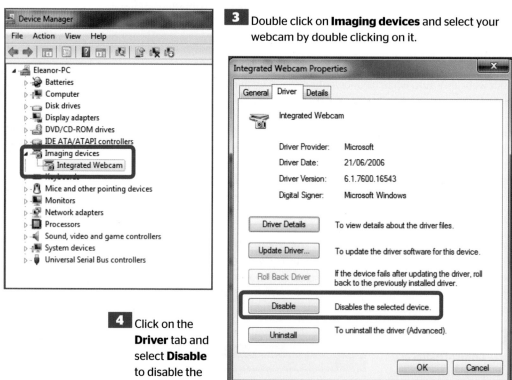

4 Click on the **Driver** tab and select **Disable** to disable the webcam.

5 Click **Yes** when asked if you really want to disable it. Your webcam is now disabled. To re-enable the webcam, simply follow the above steps and then click on **Enable** in the window that appears in Step 4.

Instant messaging

Also known as IM, instant messaging lets you send and receive real-time text messages across the internet so you can chat to selected people while online.

To use instant messaging, it's necessary to open an account with an IM program, most of which are free. There are several IM programs to download, including Yahoo! Messenger and Skype, or you can use a browser-based IM services, such as Facebook and Gmail. One of the most popular IM programs is Windows Live Messenger, available as part of Microsoft Live Essentials.

I don't want everyone on my friends list to know I'm available to chat

Windows Live Messenger lets you set and show your availability to chat to those who you're connected to. You can choose from the following: **Available**, **Busy**, **Away** or **Appear offline**.

However, sometime you may want to appear offline to some of your contacts – either individuals or groups – while continuing to show your online status to everyone else. Here's how:

1 Sign into Windows Live Messenger.

2 Right click the name of a person, group or category, and then click **Appear offline to this person**, **Appear offline to this group** or **Appear offline to this category**.

I'm not getting social updates from any of my friends

Social updates tell you what your friends are doing on other websites and on Windows Live. You should start receiving social updates automatically once you have added friends or connected to other services. To connect services:

1 Sign into Windows Live Messenger.

2 At the bottom right corner of the main 'Windows Live Messenger' window, in the 'Connected to' section, click **Add**.

3 Click **Connect more services**.

4 Click the name of a service, and then follow the instructions to connect that service.

I'm concerned about people accessing my private details

Privacy settings allow you to choose who sees your personal information such as your profile, photos and friends. You can easily change privacy settings in Live Messenger.

1 Sign into Windows Live Messenger.

2 Point to your display picture and then click **View your profile**.

3 Click **Privacy**, and then choose a level – **Private**, **Limited** or **Public**. Each one is explained in the dialog box.

4 In the 'Advanced Privacy Options', make the changes that you require.

5 Click **Save** to apply your changes.

Skype

Skype lets you place audio and even video calls between computers for free. It's very popular and is a great alternative to expensive phone calls, especially if you're calling someone overseas. Skype is a free download and requires that both people taking part in the call are using Skype. If your laptop has a webcam and you have a quick enough broadband connection, you can also place video calls for free.

However, Skype can present some problems, which can be frustrating if you need to connect to someone immediately.

Help! Skype just isn't working

Sometimes problems aren't accompanied with helpful error messages and so it can appear that Skype just doesn't seem to be working. Here are quick checks you can perform straight away to see if it really isn't working as it should be.

Check for a Skype heartbeat

If Skype is refusing to connect or not working, check the Skype service to see if it is working. If the service is down, then the problem is with the service rather than the software on your computer – all you can do is wait and hope the service resumes shortly. To check for a Skype heartbeat:

1 Click **Start**, then click **All Programs** and locate your web browser. Double click it to launch.

2 In the address bar of the web browser, type **http://heartbeat.skype.com** as the web address.

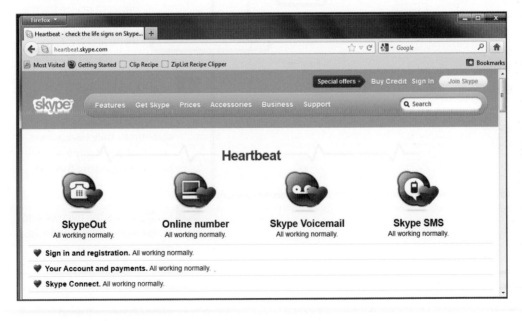

The heartbeat site lets you know if the Skype service is up and running. If it isn't, then you just need to wait for the service to restore before connecting by regularly checking the heartbeat page.

Check that the microphone and speakers are working

If you're not able to listen to or send audio, you can quickly check if the microphone on your computer is working, and the same with your speakers.

1 Launch Skype and click **Tools and Options** to display the 'Options' window. Click **Audio settings** in the left-hand column.

2 To test the microphone, speak into it – you will see an animated green bar showing the volume. If you don't see it, click the 'Microphone' **drop-down arrow** and choose another device and keep testing it until you see the green bar move.

3 To test the speakers, click **Sounds** in the left-hand column, and press the green Play button to the right of the speaker device. You should hear the Skype dialing sound – if you don't, select a different device from the 'Speakers' pop-up menu and try again until you do get sound.

4 Alternatively, check if the speakers or microphone hardware is working – sometimes they have sliders to adjust the volume or mute buttons. Make sure they are set correctly.

5 Finally, check the microphone or speakers are plugged into the correct port on your computer. USB microphones need to be plugged into the PC's USB port, while analogue microphones will need plugging into the microphone port (usually labelled with a small microphone icon).

Check your webcam drivers

It may be that your webcam is not working because it's lacking drivers and Skype can't see it. To check:

1 Launch Skype and then click **Tools and Options** to display the 'Options' window.

2 Click **Video setting** in the left-hand column. If you see a message saying 'Skype couldn't find a webcam' or 'Can't start video', then a likely cause is a lack of drivers for the webcam.

3 Visit the webcam maker's website to download and install the latest webcam drivers, then try Steps 1 and 2 again. If the message is gone, then the webcam drivers were successfully updated.

Make a test call

If you're still stumped, then try making a free test call to check if everything is working with Skype.

1 Launch Skype and then click **Tools and Options** to display the 'Options' window.

2 Click **Audio settings** from the left-hand column, and at the bottom of the window click **Make a free test call**.

3 You will be prompted to speak into the microphone after the beep. Speak clearly, and a few moments later the call will be played back to you. If you can hear the call played back, then everything is working fine. If on a regular Skype call you still can't hear the other people, then it's a problem with their end of the connection.

Shut down other programs

Skype takes up a portion of your broadband bandwidth. If you have any other programs running that are downloading or uploading to the internet, such as catch-up TV applications or streaming video downloading, this can clog your bandwidth. A tell-tale sign is voices might sound artificial and distorted. Close all other applications and try using Skype again running on its own.

When I make a call the quality seems to drop

During a Skype call, you will see a call bar displayed at the bottom of the calling area. If you can't see it, try moving your mouse around until it appears. To check your call quality settings, click the call quality icon in this bar. The 'Call Quality Settings' dialog box will open. Click on each of the five tabs in turn to fine-tune the settings for your call:

■ **Microphone** You can change the microphone that you're using by selecting a microphone from the drop-down list. To change the volume of your microphone, **move the slider** left or right. Alternatively, make sure the 'Automatically adjust microphone settings' check box is ticked to allow Skype to automatically obtain the best quality.

■ **Speakers** If necessary, adjust your speakers. To change the volume of your speakers, move the slider to the left or right. To allow Skype to automatically adjust your speaker settings for the best quality make sure that the 'Automatically adjust speaker settings' check box is ticked.
■ **Webcam** This shows a preview of the video from your webcam, along with a message about the image quality. You can change the webcam that you're using by selecting another one from the drop-down list.
■ **Computer** On this tab you will see a message indicating whether your computer speed is fast enough to maintain the call.
■ **Connection** Here you will see a message indicating whether your connection speed is fast enough for the call. In order to re-test your connection speed, click **Test now**.

I'm getting lots of problems when I make video calls

As well as basic voice communication, if you have a webcam and the person on the other end of the call also has a webcam, you can place free video calls to each other. This sounds straightforward, but you may find that you are unable to see the video or to send it.

Make sure you're not hiding

If the person you're trying to have a video call with cannot see your video, make sure that you have the correct settings to display your video.

1 Launch Skype and begin a video chat. If your friend cannot see a video of you, then look across the bottom of the video screen and locate the row of icons for the chat.

2 Look for the video icon – it looks like a small video camera. If it has a red diagonal line through it, then click it to reactivate your video stream so the other person can see you.

3 Check that the same red diagonal line is not on the icon that looks like a microphone – if it is you won't be able to be heard. Click this to remove the block on audio as well.

Check for other programs

Some other applications will also want to use your webcam, and this might result in Skype not being able to use the webcam for its own video calling. Check that the webcam light is not already on (it's usually a red or green light next to the camera lens) – if it is on before you launch Skype, then the webcam may be being used by another application.

One way to be certain is to shut down any web browsers, internet applications and instant messaging programs that may be running – all these can hijack your webcam and prevent it being used by Skype.

Check your webcam settings

If you're still experiencing problems and you have updated your webcam driver to the latest version (see page 81), then check out Skype's preferences to make sure they are set correctly.

1 Turn on the webcam, or if it came with special software, launch that and switch on the webcam to check it is working.

2 Launch Skype and click **Tools and Options** to display the 'Options' window. Click the **Video settings** on the left-hand column. If your webcam is working properly, you will see a video of yourself being shown.

3 Under the 'Automatically receive video and screen sharing from...' section, make sure the setting is not 'no one'. Instead, choose either **people in my Contact list only** or **anyone**.

4 Under the 'Show that I have video to...' make sure that the **people in my Contact list only** option is selected, rather than the 'no one' option.

This will ensure that people on your contact list can see a video of you, and you can see a video of them.

Facebook

With more than 900 million users, Facebook is the world's largest free-access social networking website. It allows users to interact with other people, find friends and join networks organised by city, workplace, school and region. You create a personal profile to share information, photos and videos to selected friends.

I can't find my friends using Facebook's search

There may be a couple of reasons why you can't find someone using search:

- Be more specific in you search. Try filtering your search results by clicking the **See more results for...** link at the bottom of the search box. Then, use the filters on the left side of the screen to narrow your results.
- Your friend may not be on Facebook yet. Send them an email inviting them to register on Facebook.
- The person you're looking for may have restricted their privacy settings or even blocked you. Sometimes this is done by mistake, so if you think this might be the case, ask your friend to check their privacy settings.

I've changed my mind about adding someone as a friend

If you change your mind about a person who you have invited to be your friend, simply cancel the friend request.

1 Go to the person's profile or timeline.

2 Hover over the **Friend Request Sent** button at the top of the page.

3 Click **Cancel Request** from the drop-down menu.

I don't want to be friends with someone. What can I do about this?

By default, anyone on Facebook can send you a friend request. You can delete a request on the Requests page by clicking the person's name and then **Delete request**. The request will be removed but the sender won't know that you have deleted their request.

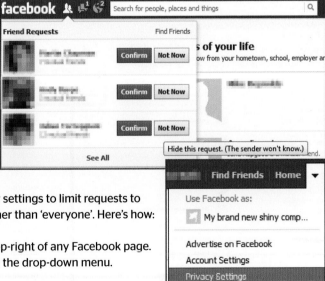

You can also use Facebook's privacy settings to limit requests to those sent by 'friends of friends' rather than 'everyone'. Here's how:

1 Click the **down arrow** at the top-right of any Facebook page. Choose **Privacy Settings** from the drop-down menu.

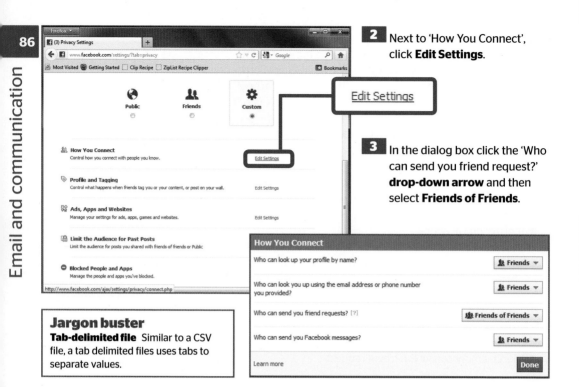

2 Next to 'How You Connect', click **Edit Settings**.

3 In the dialog box click the 'Who can send you friend request?' **drop-down arrow** and then select **Friends of Friends**.

Jargon buster
Tab-delimited file Similar to a CSV file, a tab delimited files uses tabs to separate values.

I can't import my LinkedIn contacts into Facebook

Facebook lets you import your contacts from a range of email and other accounts such as Windows Live Messenger, Gmail and Skype. You will see this feature on your 'Find Friends' page. Even if the account you want to use isn't listed – such as LinkedIn – you can still export your contacts as a CSV or tab-delimited text file and then upload this to Facebook. To do this:

1 Click on the Home page of your Facebook account, click **Find Friends** in the left-hand column, then under 'Add Personal Contacts as Friends' and click **Other Tools**.

Jargon buster
CSV file A commonly used way of moving data from one application to another, a Comma Separated Values (CSV) file is a text file that saves data (text and numbers) in an organised fashion. Also known as a Comma Delimited file, when it is opened in a word processing program, each piece of information (value) is shown separated by a comma.

2 Click **Upload Contact File**.

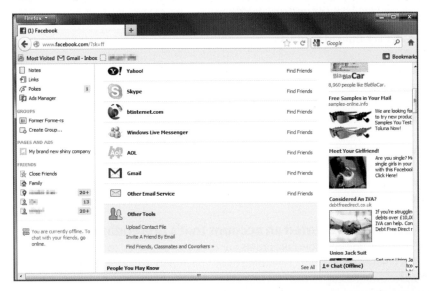

3 Click **How to create a contact file....**

How to create a contact file...

4 From the list that appears choose the program you want to use, in this case LinkedIn, and follow the instruction to create a contact file.

LinkedIn

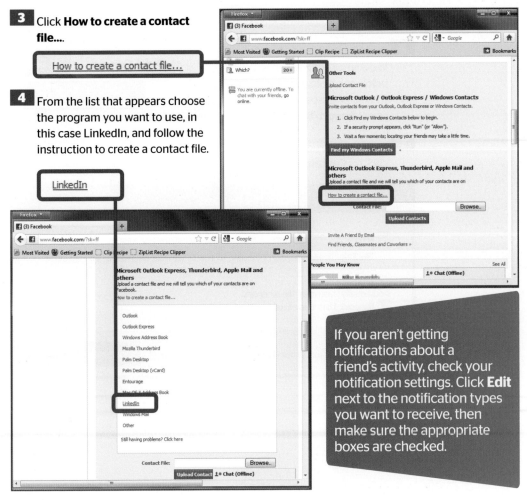

If you aren't getting notifications about a friend's activity, check your notification settings. Click **Edit** next to the notification types you want to receive, then make sure the appropriate boxes are checked.

5 To upload the file to Facebook, click **Choose File** or **Browse** and select the contact file you have just created.

6 Click **Upload Contacts**.

I can't upload my photos

If you can't upload photos to Facebook or it takes a long time, try the following:
- Make sure you have the latest version of Adobe Flash installed.
- Try uploading unedited photos. You may experience problems uploading photos that you have previously edited in a photo-editing software.
- Ensure the photo format is supported. Facebook recommends using .jpg, .bmp, .png, .gif and .tiff files.
- Ensure the photo size is less than 15MB.
- Make sure that you're using the latest version of your web browser.

Somone has created an account that's pretending to be me

Facebook doesn't allow fake profiles or impostor accounts, so if someone has created an account pretending to be you, report it at once to Facebook by following these steps:

1 Go to the profile (timeline) of the fake account.

2 Click the **Options** button (it looks like a small cog), which is just below the main photograph at the top of the page, and then select **Report/Block**.

3 Check the box next to 'Report this profile' or 'Report this timeline' and then click on **Continue**.

4 Under the section 'This profile/timeline is pretending to be someone else' place a tick next to the box labelled **Me**.

5 Click **Continue**.

6 Add a description for why you're reporting the profile (timeline), then click **Continue**.

Report and/or Block This Person

Why are you reporting this person? Please check all reasons that apply. You can review and confirm your report on the next step.

This is my old account.
☐ Recover this account, it's hacked
☐ Close this account

This person is sharing spam or inappropriate things.
☐ Spammy friend requests
☐ Spam or scam messages
☐ Other inappropriate content

This timeline is pretending to be someone else.
☑ Me
☐ Someone I know
☐ Celebrity

ent a
☐ Fake name
☐ Pet, cartoon or other character
☐ Business or organization
☐ Other

☐ Bullying or harassing

☐ Hacked account
☐ Using multiple accounts

Confirm Your Report

You're reporting ▇▇▇▇▇ timeline for the reasons below. Please review it, and remove any reasons that may not apply.

Pretending to be me   Remove this reason

This person is pretending to be me, and they are not!|

[Continue] [Cancel]

ty?   [Continue] [Cancel]

7 Check the box next to 'I confirm that this report is correct'.

8 Click **Continue** to submit your report.

I don't like the way Timeline shows my life

Designed to make it easier for yourself and others to sift through past activities, Facebook's Timeline feature displays a large cover picture at the top of a profile, then lists all posts and events below in chronological order.

If you're not happy about the way the Facebook Timeline presents your personal information to friends (or non-friends), follow these tips for tightening up your Facebook privacy settings:

1 Click the 'Home' **drop-down arrow** and then click **Privacy Settings**. Beside the heading 'Timeline and Tagging', click the blue link marked **Edit Settings**.

2 Click the **down arrow** next to 'Who can post on your Timeline', and choose 'Friends' or 'No one' for extra control. Similarly, click the **drop-down arrow** to set who is allowed to see posts on your Timeline when you're tagged.

Timeline and Tagging

Who can post on your timeline? **👥 Friends ▼**

Who can see what others post on your timeline? **⚙ Custom ▼**

- 🌐 Everyone
- 👥 Friends of Friends
- 👥 Friends
- ✓ ⚙ **Custom**
- 🖼 Close Friends
- 👤 ▬▬▬▬
- See all lists…

Review posts friends tag you in before they appear on your timeline

Who can see posts you've been tagged in on your timeline?

Review tags friends add to your own posts on Facebook

Who sees tag suggestions when photos that look like you are uploaded?

Done

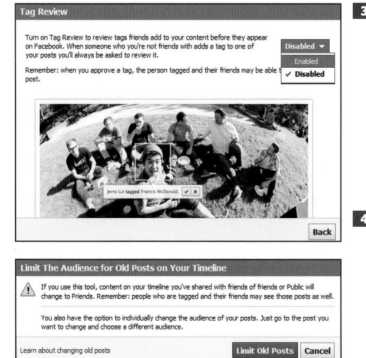

Tag Review

Turn on Tag Review to review tags friends add to your content before they appear on Facebook. When someone who you're not friends with adds a tag to one of your posts you'll always be asked to review it.

Remember: when you approve a tag, the person tagged and their friends may be able t post.

Disabled ▼

- Enabled
- ✓ **Disabled**

Jerry Lui tagged Francis McDonald. ✓ | ✕

Back

Limit The Audience for Old Posts on Your Timeline

⚠ If you use this tool, content on your timeline you've shared with friends of friends or Public will change to Friends. Remember: people who are tagged and their friends may see those posts as well.

You also have the option to individually change the audience of your posts. Just go to the post you want to change and choose a different audience.

Learn about changing old posts **Limit Old Posts** | **Cancel**

3 Adjust your settings so that you can check posts before they appear on your timeline. Where it says 'Review posts friends tag you in before they appear on your timeline' click the **arrow** (facing right) and click the **down arrow** beside the word 'Disabled'. Click **Enabled** and then click **Back**.

4 One of the biggest complaints about the Facebook Timeline is that it resurfaces old posts and photographs for all to see. To avoid this, in 'Privacy Settings', beside 'Limit the Audience for Past Posts' click **Manage Past Post Visibility**. Click **Limit Old Posts** and then click **Confirm**. Click **Close**.

Twitter

Twitter is a type of social networking site that lets you send short messages, known as 'tweets'. The subject of a tweet can be anything you want – from the serious to the humorous from conversational to simply reflecting the trivia of life.

I can't register the username I want

On Twitter, your username is your identity and shows in your tweets. However, your name may already be in use, so you will need to select a different one. Try adding characters, underscores, or abbreviations before or after the username you want to use. You can also try adding an adjective or descriptor, such as @peterthegreat or @tallterry.

If you prefer to remain anonymous, choose a more generic name or a nickname. You can list your real name in your profile if you want to provide more information to your followers.

Whichever username you choose keep it short. Twitter limits a username to just 15 characters to avoid a long name taking up too much of its 140 character limit.

Twitter is asking me to confirm an account I didn't register

Getting a confirmation email for a Twitter account you didn't sign up for may be nothing more malicious than someone simply mistyping their email (and typing yours instead) during the registration process. To remove your email from the account:

1 Click the **not my account** link that appears in the confirmation email.

2 You will be asked to confirm the removal of your email from that specific Twitter account. Click **I did not sign up for this account**. Your email address will be unlinked from the Twitter account, and you will see a confirmation screen.

I can't follow any more people!

You may have reached one of Twitter's follow limit. If you're following 2,000 other people, Twitter imposes limits on the number of additional users you can follow. This differs for each account and is based on your ratio of followers to following. If you have reached this limit, you must wait until you yourself have more followers before you can follow additional users. You can, of course, 'unfollow' some accounts to add a few additional people, but be careful as regularly following and unfollowing lots of accounts is a violation of Twitter's rules and your account may be suspended.

I can't upload a profile picture

If you can't upload a profile image to Twitter, first check the image's size and file format. The image must be a .jpg, .gif, or .png, as these are the only file formats supported by Twitter, and be no more than 700k in size. If this doesn't solve the problem, try upgrading your web browser or use another browser. Finally make sure you click **Save changes** at the bottom of your 'Settings' page otherwise your profile won't be updated.

Help! My Direct Message was posted to my public timeline

A Direct Message (DM) is a private message that only you and the recipient can see. To send a DM, go to the **Profile** page of the user you want to contact, and click on the **Person** icon and select **Send a Direct Message**. In the pop-up window, type your DM and click **Send**. However, a quicker method is simply to put 'd' followed by the username and message text into the status update box, for example, 'dwhichtech Really enjoyed listening to your latest podcast'.

If a DM appears on your public timeline, it's most likely because you haven't included 'd username' at the beginning of the message. This means Twitter sees it as a public tweet, not a direct message. To delete it from your timeline, click on the message and then click **Delete** at the bottom of the tweet. A message will pop up asking you to confirm by clicking **Delete Tweet**.

Why aren't my hashtags (#) working?

Hashtags, denoted using the # symbol before a word, are used to mark topics in a tweet, and can be used to categorise tweets. They help show the most popular topics that people are tweeting about. This is useful if you want to search for tweets on a topic – perhaps a major news event such as #planecrash or #DiamondJubilee. Clicking on a hashtag brings up a screen showing search results for all other tweets that include that hashtag.

If you're having trouble using hashtags, it may be a result of punctuation. Punctuation marks (, . ; ' ? ! etc.) end a hashtag wherever they occur, so if you write **#nowewon't** the message will be categorised as **#nowewon**. Also make sure the # symbol has a space directly in front of it otherwise it won't show correctly in searches. Finally, avoid creating hashtags that consist entirely of numbers such as **#1**, as they won't be searchable.

Part of my profile image gets chopped off when it's uploaded

Twitter displays profile pictures as small squares. So if you upload a picture that's rectangular, Twitter crops it so it's a square. You can control what's shown in the image by first editing the image's dimensions in an image editor such as Windows Photo Gallery before you upload it to Twitter.

I've tweeted something by mistake, what can I do?

If you make a mistake or regret a tweet, you can delete it. Simply hover over the tweet on your Profile page, and click the **Delete** button. This removes it from your followers' timelines, but there's nothing you can do if other users have already retweeted it. That's the power of Twitter, so think carefully before you tweet something you may regret later.

One of my followers is posting rude and offensive tweets that I don't want to see

If someone is posting harassing comments or tweets that make you uncomfortable, use Twitter's blocking feature. By blocking a follower, you remove their tweets from your own timeline and they won't be able to follow you. They may still be able to view your tweets by going directly to your Twitter page, but they will not show up automatically. They also won't be able to send you direct messages nor will they appear in your list of followers. To block a Twitter user:

1 Log in to your Twitter account and go to the Profile page of the person you wish to block.

2 Click the **Person** icon next to the name of the person you want to block.

3 From the drop-down menu click **Block @ username** (where 'username' is the name of the person following you) from the options listed.

I've added a website link to my Tweet but now there's no space for my text!

Website links (URLs) can be very long, for example the full link to a Which? Best Buy laptops is: http://www.which.co.uk/technology/computing/reviews/laptops/best-buy/verdict/. Pasting this link into a tweet would leave very little space for your words. The solution is to use a URL shortener. This is a service that takes the original long URL and makes it much shorter, while still taking you to the same place when it's clicked. One of the most popular URL shortening websites is bitly.

1 Open your web browser and type **https://bitly.com/** into the address bar and click Enter on your keyboard.

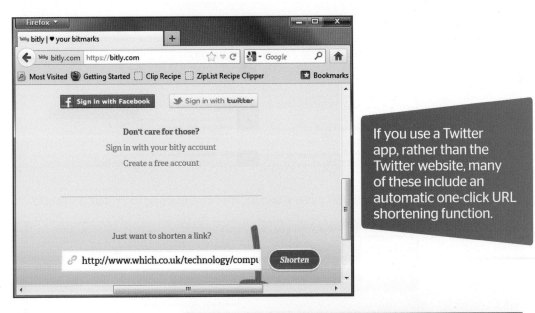

If you use a Twitter app, rather than the Twitter website, many of these include an automatic one-click URL shortening function.

2 Type or paste the long URL into the box on the bitly website.

3 Click the **Shorten** button.

4 Copy the short URL and paste it into your tweet.

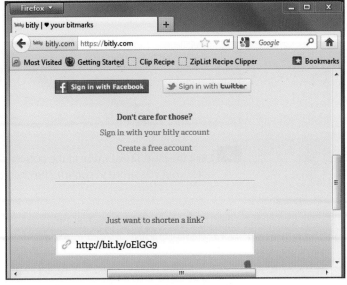

I don't want my tweets to be read by everyone. What can I do?

If the thought of your tweets being freely available for anyone in the world to read makes you uncomfortable, you can select to protect them. Protected tweets are only visible to Twitter followers you have previously approved. To protect your tweets:

1 Click the **Person** icon at the top-right corner of your profile page and from the drop-down menu select **Settings**.

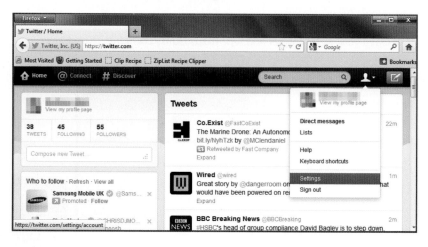

2 In the 'Tweet privacy' section, check the box next to 'Protect my tweets'.

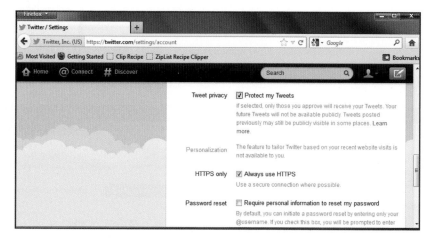

3 Click the blue **Save** button at the bottom of the page. You will be asked to enter your password to confirm the change.

Internet and web problems

By reading this chapter you'll get to grips with:

- Fixing common browser problems
- Choosing good usernames and strong passwords
- Using online storage services to share files

Browser error messages explained

If confusing error messages stop you dead in your tracks, here's a guide with a threat rating for each of the common error messages you might come across, so you will know exactly what to do.

I've got a warning about an unsafe or forged website

Browser alert: Web forgery

Threat rating: High – stop and take notice, you need to act

If you see a warning message, 'This site has been reported unsafe' or 'Reported Web Forgery', it's likely that you have inadvertently landed on a phishing website and your browser's phishing filter has blocked its content. Phishing sites are fake websites that often look like banking sites or other recognised institutions. They're designed by scammers to extract money and personal information from you. Luckily, most browsers have phishing filters built in these days. See pages 109–10 for how to check these are turned on.

My browser keeps displaying a message to update it

Browser alert: Update required

Threat rating: Medium – read the message carefully, then proceed

If using Internet Explorer (IE), you're unlikely to see this message as updates for IE are handled via Windows Updates. Assuming you have 'Automatic Updates' switched on (see page 205), you shouldn't have to manually update your browser. Other browsers, including Firefox and Google Chrome, will occasionally need updating to stay secure. By default, your browser should be set to download new updates as they become available. Firefox, for example, will check for and retrieve the latest updates in the background. Next time you start the browser it will present you with an alert saying that the new version needs to be installed. Follow the prompts.

I get an alert saying that pop-ups are blocked

Browser alert: Pop-up blocked

Threat rating: Low – a benign alert, OK to continue

Pop-ups are small windows that appear while you surf the web. Most are adverts but some can contain malicious links or unsuitable material. Most browsers these days come with built-in pop-up blockers that are activated by default. See pages 99–101 to learn how to check whether your browser's pop-up blocker is switched on and how to allow pop-ups for specific sites. Your browser will display an alert informing you that it has blocked a pop-up – usually along the top edge of the web page. Most of the time you can just ignore these messages.

I can't see interactive or video content on a web page

Browser alert: Plug-in required

Threat rating: Medium – read the message carefully, then proceed

Most browsers use plug-ins (or add-ons) in order to add some kind of functionality. The most common plug-in is Adobe's Flash Player, which lets you view video content embedded in many web pages. If you don't have the correct plug-in installed, this will generate an error message on-screen. In the case of Flash, you can follow the on-screen links to download the plug-in, but don't install plug-ins from sources you don't know. Some companies use Flash to track your online behaviour.

Dealing with pop-ups

Pop-ups are additional browser windows that are opened by a website. Often simply annoying, as they're frequently used to push advertisements at the viewer, pop-ups can also be harmful. Pop-ups can contain malicious links or unsuitable material. Most browsers these days come with filters that automatically block pop-ups and with controls so you can allow pop-ups from benign sites.

I want to block pop-ups

You can stop pop-ups from appearing by using your browser's settings or preferences. Here's how in Internet Explorer:

1 Click **Tools** and then click **Internet options** from the drop-down menu.

2 In the 'Internet Options' dialog box, click the **Privacy** tab.

Not all pop-ups are malicious. Some websites legitimately use pop-up windows to provide information or instructions (such as downloading content or tick boxes for agreeing to terms and conditions) on the current webpage so that you don't have to click through to a different page.

Internet Options

General | Security | **Privacy** | Content | Connections | Programs | Advanced

Settings

Select a setting for the Internet zone.

Medium

- Blocks third-party cookies that do not have a compact privacy policy
- Blocks third-party cookies that save information that can be used to contact you without your explicit consent
- Restricts first-party cookies that save information that can be used to contact you without your implicit consent

Sites | Import | Advanced | Default

Location

☐ Never allow websites to request your physical location | Clear Sites

Pop-up Blocker

☑ Turn on Pop-up Blocker | Settings

InPrivate

☑ Disable toolbars and extensions when InPrivate Browsing starts

OK | Cancel | Apply

3 Make sure the check box next to 'Turn on Pop-up Blocker' is ticked. To allow pop-ups from a specific site, click the **Settings** button.

4 In the window that opens, type the address of the site in the 'Address of website to allow' field and click **Add**.

Address of website to allow:

http://www.amazon.co.uk/ | Add

Pop-up Blocker Settings

Exceptions

Pop-ups are currently blocked. You can allow pop-ups from specific websites by adding the site to the list below.

Address of website to allow:

http://www.amazon.co.uk/ | Add

Allowed sites:

http://support.euro.dell.com/support/index.aspx?c=uk&... | Remove
http://www1.euro.dell.com/content/default.aspx?c=uk... | Remove all...

Notifications and blocking level:

☑ Play a sound when a pop-up is blocked.
☑ Show Notification bar when a pop-up is blocked.

Blocking level:

Medium: Block most automatic pop-ups

Learn more about Pop-up Blocker | Close

5 Click **Close**.

Here's how in Firefox:

1 Click **Firefox** in the top-left corner and then, from the drop-down menu, click **Options**.

Firefox ▾

New Tab ▸ | ☆ Bookmarks ▸
Start Private Browsing | History ▸
Edit ▸ | Downloads
Find... | Add-ons
Save Page As... | Options ▸ | Options
Send Link... | Help ▸ | Menu Bar
Print... ▸ | | ✓ Navigation Toolbar
Web Developer ▸ | | Bookmarks Toolbar
Full Screen | | ✓ Add-on Bar   Ctrl+/
Set Up Sync... | | ✓ Tabs on Top
Exit | | Toolbar Layout...

&oe=utf-8&aq=t&rls=org.mozilla:en-US:official&client=firefo

lews   Gmail   More ▾

www.google.co.uk/

Images
Maps
Videos

The local version of this pre-eminent search engine, offering UK-specific pages as well world results.

Google Maps
Zoomable maps focused on an address or post code. Maps can

Google Images
Google Images. The most comprehensive image search

2 In the dialog box that appears, click on the **Content** tab.

3 Make sure there's a tick next to 'Block pop-up windows'.

Options

| General | Tabs | Content | Applications | Privacy | Security | Sync | Advanced |

☑ Block pop-up windows   Exceptions...

☑ Load images automatically   Exceptions...

☑ Enable JavaScript   Advanced...

Fonts & Colors

Default font: Times New Roman ▼ Size: 16 ▼   Advanced...

Colors...

Languages

Choose your preferred language for displaying pages   Choose...

OK   Cancel   Help

4 Click on the **Exceptions...** button next to the Block pop-up option and type the address of a website that you wish to allow pop-ups for.

5 Click **Allow**, and then click **Close** and **OK** to finish.

Use the exceptions button for sites you use on a regular basis that rely on pop-ups for other, more innocent reasons. For example, some webmail packages use pop-ups for composing new messages.

Allowed Sites - Pop-ups

You can specify which websites are allowed to open pop-up windows. Type the exact address of the site you want to allow and then click Allow.

Address of website:

http://www.amazon.co.uk

Allow

| Site | Status |
| trials.adobe.com | Allow |

Remove Site   Remove All Sites   Close

Protect your online identity

All internet browsers collect personal information about what you do and where you go online by using cookies, for example (see page 104). For instance they use cookies and browsers also keep records of the web pages that you visit in their history files.

While cookies and history files have their uses they can expose your personal information to fraudsters. Armed with a few choice facts about you, an ID thief might be able to open a bank account in your name or, worse, access your bank or credit card account. A criminal could run up debts, apply for benefits or even attempt to obtain a passport or driver's licence in your name.

How do I delete my browser history?

If you're using a public PC (in a library or cybercafé, say) to go online, it's wise to clear your browser history when you're finished.

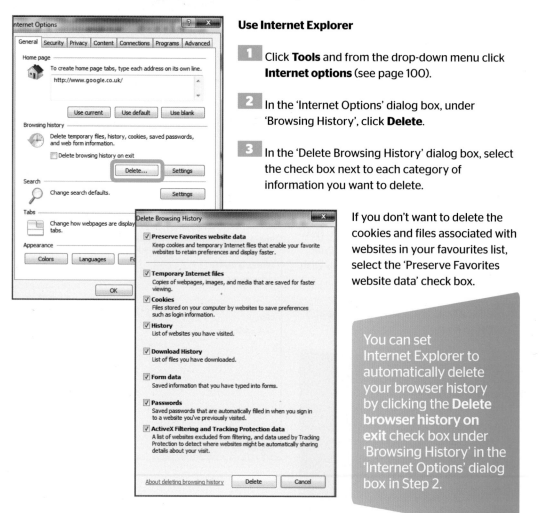

Use Internet Explorer

1 Click **Tools** and from the drop-down menu click **Internet options** (see page 100).

2 In the 'Internet Options' dialog box, under 'Browsing History', click **Delete**.

3 In the 'Delete Browsing History' dialog box, select the check box next to each category of information you want to delete.

If you don't want to delete the cookies and files associated with websites in your favourites list, select the 'Preserve Favorites website data' check box.

You can set Internet Explorer to automatically delete your browser history by clicking the **Delete browser history on exit** check box under 'Browsing History' in the 'Internet Options' dialog box in Step 2.

Use Firefox

1 Click **Tools** and then **Options**.

2 In the 'Options' dialog box, click the **Privacy** tab.

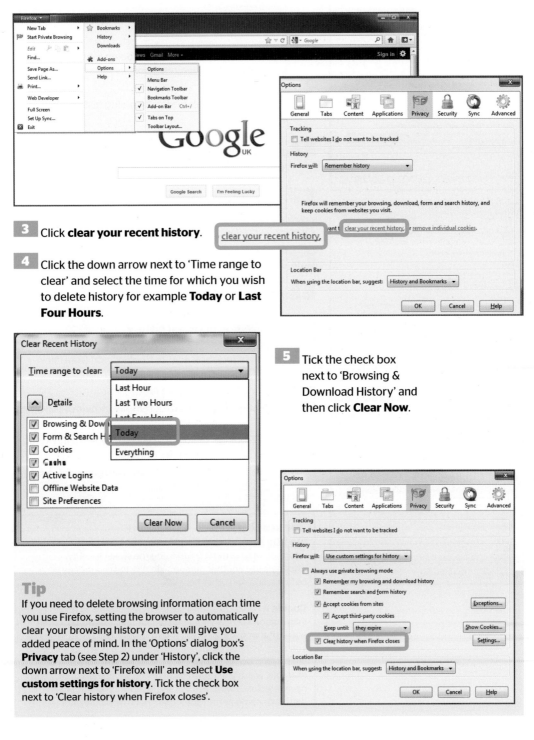

3 Click **clear your recent history**.

4 Click the down arrow next to 'Time range to clear' and select the time for which you wish to delete history for example **Today** or **Last Four Hours**.

5 Tick the check box next to 'Browsing & Download History' and then click **Clear Now**.

Tip

If you need to delete browsing information each time you use Firefox, setting the browser to automatically clear your browsing history on exit will give you added peace of mind. In the 'Options' dialog box's **Privacy** tab (see Step 2) under 'History', click the down arrow next to 'Firefox will' and select **Use custom settings for history**. Tick the check box next to 'Clear history when Firefox closes'.

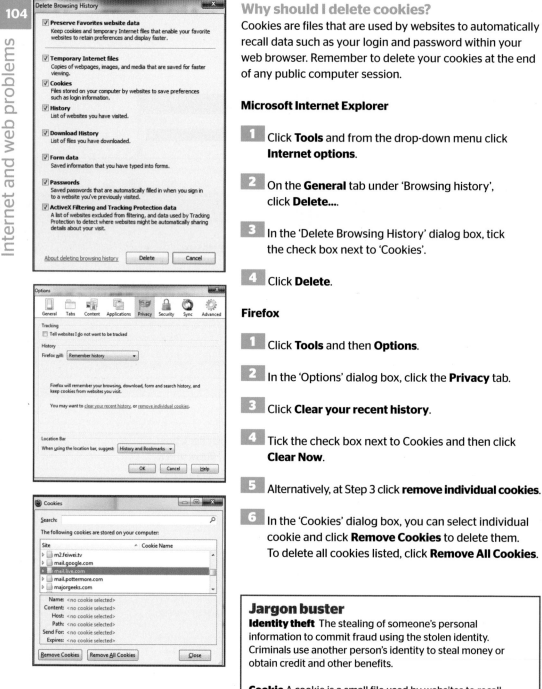

Why should I delete cookies?

Cookies are files that are used by websites to automatically recall data such as your login and password within your web browser. Remember to delete your cookies at the end of any public computer session.

Microsoft Internet Explorer

1 Click **Tools** and from the drop-down menu click **Internet options**.

2 On the **General** tab under 'Browsing history', click **Delete...**.

3 In the 'Delete Browsing History' dialog box, tick the check box next to 'Cookies'.

4 Click **Delete**.

Firefox

1 Click **Tools** and then **Options**.

2 In the 'Options' dialog box, click the **Privacy** tab.

3 Click **Clear your recent history**.

4 Tick the check box next to Cookies and then click **Clear Now**.

5 Alternatively, at Step 3 click **remove individual cookies**.

6 In the 'Cookies' dialog box, you can select individual cookie and click **Remove Cookies** to delete them. To delete all cookies listed, click **Remove All Cookies**.

Jargon buster

Identity theft The stealing of someone's personal information to commit fraud using the stolen identity. Criminals use another person's identity to steal money or obtain credit and other benefits.

Cookie A cookie is a small file used by websites to recall information such as your login details and passwords. When you visit a website, a cookie is sent to your computer. When you next visit that particular site this cookie is sent back by your web browser so that the site can 'remember you'. For example, when you return to an online shopping site that you have registered with, you will see 'Hello John Smith [insert your own name here]' rather than 'Hello new customer'.

Usernames and passwords

With more and more online services demanding a username and password – from sending an email or shopping online, to paying your Council Tax – creating and then keeping track of your login details without sacrificing their all-important security can be quite a challenge.

I'm worried that my password won't be strong enough

Good passwords are the key to keeping our personal data safe. Many people use things like their mother's maiden name, but you might be surprised to learn just how easy it is to find out information like this from public records, for example.

It can be difficult to remember multiple passwords, but you could consider adopting a three-tiered password system where you have different levels of password for different types of website:
- **Low security** For signing up for a newsletter.
- **Medium security** For webmail and instant messenger services.
- **High security** For anything where your personal finance is involved.

For a high-security password, a series of randomly generated letters and numbers is best, but if you needed something to help you remember your password by, you could consider creating your password from something such as the first letter of each word in a line from a favourite song.

> **Tip**
> A username can be anything you want but it's best to keep it short and memorable. It can be your full name, part of your name or a fictitious one. You may prefer not to use your full name as this could identify you. And, if your first choice of username has already been taken – as can be the case if a website has lots of members – try a variation or add some numbers such as 'jjones56'. Some websites, particularly online shops, may ask for your email address rather than a username.

I'm not sure if it's safe to save login details

Some websites and services give you the option to save your login details. This avoids the need to enter your username and password every time you want to access the site or service.

However, you should only consider doing this if you use your own home or personal computer to access a website. Saving such information to a shared PC is a security risk, particularly on a public computer.

Some sites, Hotmail for example, offer an option to save just your email address. This is appropriate for home use, but if you're using a public PC ensure that the 'Always ask for my email address and password' box (or equivalent) is checked.

Help, I have forgotten my username and password for a website

With so many websites requiring a username and password to login, trying to remember the correct information for each one can be difficult. Most web browsers offer autocomplete – a feature whereby the browser 'remembers' what you enter into online forms and will fill in those details automatically when you visit the specific website again. You will be able to see the username and the password will be input as normal using asterisks. Some web browsers such as Firefox also allow you store saved usernames and passwords as typed, so that if you forget one you can pull up a list in your browser and copy it from there. Here's how to do it using Firefox:

1 Go to **Tools** and from the drop-down menu click **Options**.

2 In the 'Options' dialog box click on the **Security** tab. Put a tick next to 'Remember passwords for sites.

3 To view passwords click **Saved Passwords...**. A dialog box will open that lists the address of websites using saved passwords with the corresponding username and password.

4 To ensure that only you have access to the list of 'Saved Passwords', tick the **Use a master password** check box. In the window that appears, enter your password twice and click **OK** and then **OK** again.

Change Master Password   ✕

A Master Password is used to protect sensitive information like site passwords. If you create a Master Password you will be asked to enter it once per session when Firefox retrieves saved information protected by the password.

Current password: (not set)

Enter new password: |

Re-enter password:

Password quality meter

Please make sure you remember the Master Password you have set. If you forget your Master Password, you will be unable to access any of the information protected by it.

OK   Cancel

5 To turn off Firefox's Autocomplete feature, click **Tools** and then click **Internet Options**. Select the 'Privacy' panel and click the 'Firefox will' **drop-down arrow** and set it to **Use custom settings for history**.

6 Remove the tick from the check box that says 'Remember search and form history'. Click **OK**.

Options   ✕

General   Tabs   Content   Applications   **Privacy**   Security   Sync   Advanced

Tracking
☐ Tell websites I do not want to be tracked

History
Firefox will: Use custom settings for history   ▾

☐ Always use private browsing mode
  ☑ Remember my browsing and download history
  ☐ Remember search and form history
  ☑ Accept cookies from sites   Exceptions...
    ☑ Accept third-party cookies
    Keep until: they expire   ▾   Show Cookies...
  ☐ Clear history when Firefox closes   Settings...

Location Bar
When using the location bar, suggest: History and Bookmarks   ▾

OK   Cancel   Help

Help, I can't see my saved passwords in Internet Explorer

Internet Explorer no longer has a password manager feature. However, it will still remember usernames and passwords on websites and then fill these automatically when you revisit the site. To allow this you need to activate it in Explorer's AutoComplete options. Here's how:

1 Click **Tools** and from the drop-down menu click **Internet options**.

2 Click the **Content** tab, and under 'AutoComplete', click **Settings**.

3 Make sure the check boxes next to 'Forms', 'Usernames and passwords in forms' and 'Ask me before saving passwords' are all ticked. If you want to turn off AutoComplete click to remove the ticks from the three check boxes.

4 Click **OK** and then **OK** again.

Phishing and viruses

Adware, spyware and other malicious software (malware) from online sources can invade your privacy and, in some cases, monitor keystrokes, hijack your email or use your identity to mail out spam. Anti-virus and anti-spyware protection is an absolute must on your home PC. Similarly, a firewall will help to prevent anything from getting onto your computer. See page 212 to learn how to turn on Windows 7's firewall.

How do I protect myself against phishing scams?

Phishing is a type of email scam where you are tricked into giving away personal details by being directed to a spoof website that resembles the site of a legitimate company such as a bank. The best thing is to delete suspicious emails. You can also use phishing filters within your web browser to help you spot spoof websites.

Internet Explorer

1 Click **Tools** and click **Safety** and then **Turn on SmartScreen Filter...**.

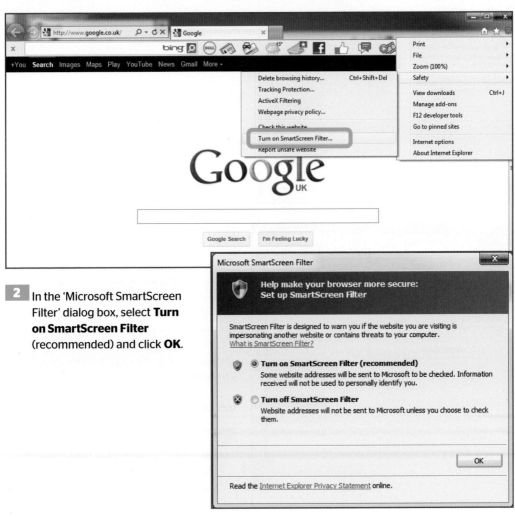

2 In the 'Microsoft SmartScreen Filter' dialog box, select **Turn on SmartScreen Filter** (recommended) and click **OK**.

Firefox

1 Click **Tools** and from the drop-down menu click **Options**.

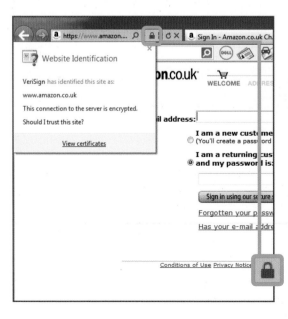

2 In the 'Internet Options' dialog box click **Security**.

3 Make sure there is a tick in the check boxes next to: 'Block reported attack sites' and 'Block reported web forgeries'.

How can I be sure a website is safe to use?

A secure website will be prefaced 'https://' rather than the usual 'http://' – the extra 's' standing for 'secure'. In Internet Explorer and Firefox, a padlock icon also appears in the address bar every time you arrive at a secure page. You can also check the security certificate for a web page to make sure that it's genuine.

Internet Explorer

1 Click the **Security Report** icon (it looks like a padlock) to the right of the website address bar. A small window will pop up giving details of the website's security certificate if it has one.

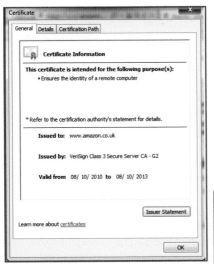

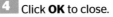 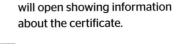

2 Click **View certificates** at the foot of the window that pops up.

3 The 'Certificate' dialog box will open showing information about the certificate.

4 Click **OK** to close.

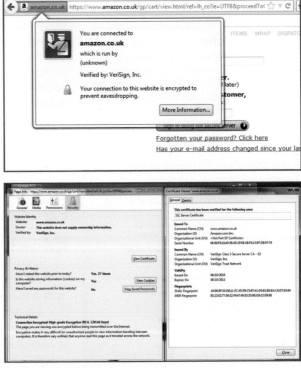

Firefox

1 Click on the **Website** icon or name to the left of the address bar. A small window will pop up giving details of the website's security certificate if it has one.

2 Click **More Information**.

3 Click the **Security** tab. Here you will see more information about the website identity and the level of encryption used. If the site has a security certificate, the name of the agency that issued the certificate will be listed under 'Website Identity'. Click **View Certificate** to see the certificate.

4 Click **Close** and then click the red **X** icon at the top right of the window.

I'd like to open a website I know is safe, but see the message 'There is a problem with this website's security certificate'

Security certificate warnings are designed to alert you to suspicious websites that attempt to fool you or steal personal data that you enter. However, if you see this message on a website that you know is genuine and trustworthy, the most likely reason is that your computer's date and time settings are incorrect. Security certificates have a 'valid from' and 'valid to' date. Typically certificates are valid for a year or two and then the company running the website must get a new certificate to keep the site secure. If your computer's date is set to a time in the past, Explorer will think the certificate is invalid and so will show the error message. To check your computer's date and time settings see pages 48-9.

Common Internet Explorer problems

Internet Explorer is Microsoft's web browser that's used to view webpages and content online. Like any web browser, however, you may encounter issues or problems that need to be resolved so you can get on with surfing the web.

I can't view a video in full screen in Internet Explorer

There are several reasons why you might encounter problems viewing a video in Internet Explorer. First, most videos use Silverlight, Flash or Java, which require add-ons to be installed in Explorer for them to play. Making sure that you have the latest updates for Windows, Internet Explorer and any Internet Explorer add-ons you have installed can usually resolve most playback issues.

But, if you're still having problems, try disabling or enabling hardware acceleration. Hardware acceleration is a new feature in Internet Explorer that moves graphics and text rendering from the computer's central processing unit (CPU) to its graphics processing unit (GPU) so that a website's performance is faster and smoother. However, you may need to turn on or disable hardware acceleration to avoid compatibility issues with viewing certain websites, particularly those with streaming or full-screen video.

Jargon buster

Graphics rendering The computer process of generating an image on screen through the translating of the programming code that describes the image – essentially drawing the image on the screen.

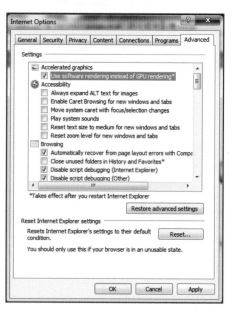

To change the hardware acceleration setting, follow these steps:

1 Click **Start**, then click **Internet Explorer**.

2 Click the **Tools** icon in the upper-right corner, and then click **Internet Options**.

3 In the resulting dialog box, click the **Advanced** tab, and then under 'Accelerated graphics', do one of the following:

- To disable hardware acceleration, tick the 'Use software rendering instead of GPU rendering' check box.
- To enable hardware acceleration, clear the 'Use software rendering instead of GPU rendering' check box.

4 Click **Apply**, and then click **OK**.

5 Close Internet Explorer and then restart it to apply the change.

Now I've upgraded to Internet Explorer 9, one of my favourite websites looks different and I can't sign in

If a website doesn't display properly or you can't perform functions such as signing into a site with a username and password, try one or more of the following options:

- Turn on Compatibility View.
- Turn off Tracking Protection.
- Turn off ActiveX Filtering.

Compatibility View

Websites that haven't been designed or optimised for Internet Explorer 9 may not display correctly. However, you can often improve how a website looks by using a feature called 'Compatibility View'. This shows the website as if you were viewing it using an earlier version of Internet Explorer.

If Internet Explorer sees a webpage that isn't compatible, it displays a 'Compatibility View' button on the Address bar. To turn on 'Compatibility View', click this button. The icon will change from an outline to a solid colour.

Now every time you visit this website, it will be displayed in 'Compatibility View'. If the website is updated to display correctly in the current version of Internet Explorer, 'Compatibility View' will automatically turn off. You can also manually turn off 'Compatibility View' when visiting a site by clicking on the Compatibility View button to uncheck it.

Tracking Protection

A new security feature in Internet Explorer 9, 'Tracking Protection' prevents websites from keeping track of your online activity. It blocks this content from websites that appear on 'Tracking Protection Lists'. Internet Explorer 9 includes a personalised list, which is generated automatically based on the sites you visit. In addition, you can download pre-configured 'Tracking Protection Lists' from the Internet Explorer Gallery. Internet Explorer will then periodically check for updates to these lists. To turn on 'Tracking Protection':

1 Click **Start**, then click **All Programs** and from the list click **Internet Explorer** to open the browser.

2 Click **Tools**, point to 'Safety', and then click **Tracking Protection...**.

3 In the 'Manage Add-ons' dialog box, click **Tracking Protection**, and then click **Enable**.

If a website doesn't display properly, you can turn off 'Tracking Protection' for this site to see if it solves the problem. In Internet Explorer, navigate to the website in question, click the **filter button** in the Address bar, and then click **Disable Tracking Protection**.

ActiveX Filtering

You may need to turn off ActiveX Filtering for this particular website. ActiveX is a technology used for interactive content on websites. As you browse the Web, you may come across web pages that won't work properly unless you have an ActiveX browser plug-in installed. You will usually be asked for your permission before an ActiveX plug-in is installed. These plug-ins, however, can pose a security risk. In some cases, they can be used to collect information, install software on your computer without your consent, or allow someone else to control your computer.

BE CAREFUL!

Avoid installing ActiveX plug-ins unless you trust the website and know exactly what the plug-in will do. The website should provide this information along with any special details you need to know before you install it.

With Internet Explorer 9, however, you can use 'ActiveX Filtering' to block ActiveX controls for all websites, and then deactivate it only for the sites that you trust. To turn on ActiveX Filtering:

1 Click the **Start** button and then click **All Programs** and from list click **Internet Explorer** to open the browser.

2 Click **Tools**, point to 'Safety' and then click **ActiveX Filtering**.

Turn off ActiveX filtering for a specific website

1 In Internet Explorer 9 navigate to a website.

2 Click the **filter button** in the Address bar.

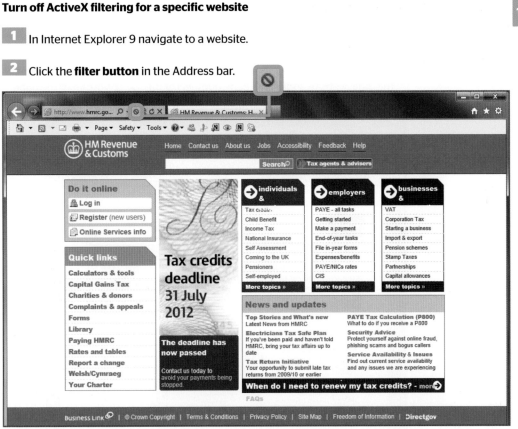

3 Turn off or turn on available filtering options for the website.

When I try to print a web page it just doesn't work

You can use Internet Explorer's 'Print preview' to see how a webpage will appear when printed and to make adjustments to improve its appearance.

1 With the website you want to print open in Internet Explorer, click **Tools**, point to 'Print', and then click **Print preview…**.

2 If you want to print a specific page, click the **Next Page** button or the **Previous Page** button at the foot of the page to find the page.

3 Click **Page Setup** to open the 'Page Setup' dialog box. Here you can make further changes including:
- Under 'Page Setup' change paper size, orientation or margins. Tick the check box by 'Enable Shrink-to-Fit' so the printed page will fill the page size.
- Under 'Headers and Footers', choose to print additional information (such as the date, website address or page number) at the top or bottom of the page.

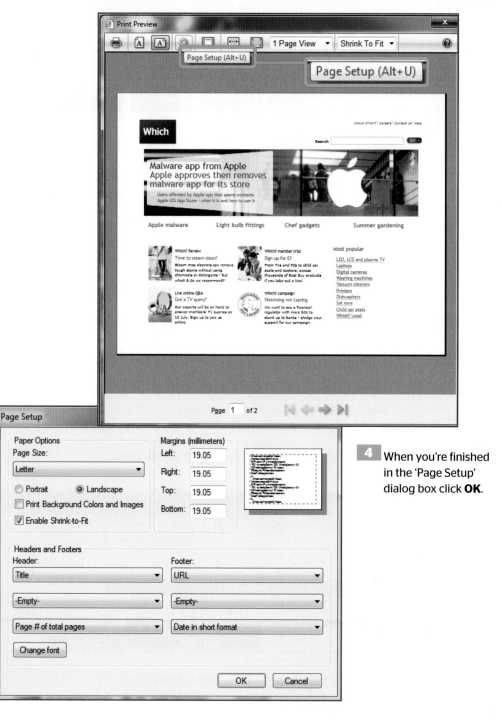

4 When you're finished in the 'Page Setup' dialog box click **OK**.

5 Click the **Print Document** button.

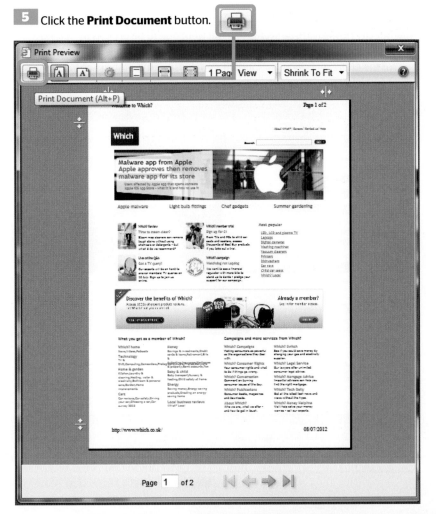

When I print a webpage the text is too small

When you print a webpage, Internet Explorer shrinks the content of the webpage to fit the width of your paper. If the webpage is wide, reducing the text size to fit the page can cause the text to be so small it's unreadable. To fix this, try changing the print size:

1 Click the **Tools** button, point to 'Print', and then click **Print preview....** From the 'Change Print Size' drop-down menu, choose **Custom**.

2 Specify how large you would like the webpage to be printed by setting a percentage in the **Custom Size** text box. This will enlarge the printed size of the entire webpage, although it might also result in some of the webpage being cut off on the printed document.

I can't read the text on a webpage once I've printed it

You can improve the legibility of a printed webpage by stopping Internet Explorer from printing background colours and images.

1 In Internet Explorer, click the **Tools** button, point to 'Print', and then click **Page setup...**.

2 Clear the 'Print Background Colors' and Images check box.

3 Click **OK**.

Online storage: SkyDrive

When using a computer with a digital camera and camcorder it's easy to quickly accumulate lots of photos and video, and for many users finding enough storage space to hold all this data is a real challenge. Many people choose to expand their storage with an external hard drive, others prefer to use compact discs or DVDs. Yet, another option that's becoming increasingly popular is cloud storage.

When you sign up to an online backup or storage service, you are given a username and password so that only you can access your data. You select which files and folders you want to save and then upload them via your internet connection to your chosen online storage provider.

> ## Jargon buster
> **Cloud storage** Nothing to do with the weather, cloud storage refers to online backup or storage services that host a copy of your files and folders on giant computers known as servers. These are remote from your computer and you access them via the internet.

It also means you will be able to access the files from other computers or devices such as a smartphone or to share it with others if you wish.

There are lots of different cloud storage systems. Some have a very specific focus, such as storing digital photographs, but the most popular ones offer a certain amount of free storage for any type of files. These include Microsoft SkyDrive, Dropbox and Google Drive.

I'm trying to upload a file but keep getting an error message

Your file may be unable to upload for one of the following reasons:
- There was an error with SkyDrive. Try to upload the file again.
- The file is too big. Files must be 300MB or less.
- Does the file have the same name as a subfolder in the folder that you're trying to upload the file to? If so, rename the file or subfolder, and then try to upload again.
- You don't have permission to upload to the folder that you have selected. Choose a folder you have permission for, and then try to upload the file again.
- You can't add files with identical names to the list of files to be uploaded. Rename the file and try to upload again.
- Uploading the file may cause your account to exceed the total storage limit. Look at the storage meter on the SkyDrive website to see how much storage space you have remaining. To free up more space, delete files that you no longer need, or use a file compression program to make the file smaller, and then try to upload the file again.
- The folder path may be too long. The entire folder path, including the file name, must contain fewer than 255 characters. Shorten the name of your file or the name of subfolders in SkyDrive, or select a subfolder that is closer to the top-level folder, and then try to upload the file again.

■ The file name has characters that aren't compatible with Windows. These are:
/ (forward slash)
\ (backslash)
| (vertical bar)
* (asterisk)
? (question mark)
: (colon)
< (less than)
> (greater than)
" (double quote)

> **Jargon buster**
> **File compression** The act of reducing the size of one or more files using a special compression program so that they can be more easily stored or transferred across the internet.

Rename the file to remove these characters, and then try to upload it again.

■ You can't upload folders directly on the SkyDrive website. You need to first create the folder and then upload your files to it. However, if you have the SkyDrive app installed, you can upload folders by adding them to the SkyDrive folder on your computer.

I can't access SkyDrive on my smartphone

You should be able to access your SkyDrive account on any smartphone, although how easily you can do this will depend on the type of smartphone you have. If you have a Windows Phone, any photos saved to your SkyDrive account automatically appear in the Pictures hub on your phone. You can also download the SkyDrive app, so that you can manage your files on your phone. Apple iPhone and iPad users can also download a free app to get easy access to their SkyDrive files on the go. If you have an Android or another type of smartphone, you can still access files on your SkyDrive, but you will need to use the browser to go to SkyDrive.com.

I've uploaded a video to SkyDrive but can't play it

Most web browsers can play Windows Media Video (.wmv files) and .mp4 videos directly from SkyDrive but you might also need to have Microsoft's Silverlight plug-in installed to play the video. You can upload other video formats to SkyDrive, but often these cannot be directly played in a browser and must be first downloaded to a computer.

Another consideration is file size – any video you upload to SkyDrive must be smaller than 300MB.

> **Jargon buster**
>
> **Silverlight** Microsoft Silverlight is a free web-browser plug-in that allows you to see video, animation and interactive content on web pages.

I can't post a link to my photos on SkyDrive

1 Sign into SkyDrive.

2 Go to the folder, photo or file you want to share and expand the rightmost pane if it has collapsed.

3 Under 'Sharing', click **Share** or **Share folder**.

4 Click the **Get a link** tab, choose link type and permission level. Permissions for your files or folder are automatically updated once you get a link.

Send email	Get a link to "My Album" ✕
Post to **f** ✈ **in**	**View only**
	Only people with this link can see the files that you share.
Get a link	Create
	View and edit
	Only people with this link can see and edit the files that you share.
	Create
	Public
	Anyone can search for and view your public files, even if you don't share a link.
Help me choose how to share	Make public

■ **View only** People who follow this link can only view your files or folder. It is important to remember that anyone who has this link will be able to view your files or folder, not just the people with whom you share the link. So if someone shares the link again, people you might not intend to share your files or folders with will have access to them.

■ **View and edit** People with this link can view the files it links to, and if they sign in, they'll also be able to edit them. The people who sign in to edit your files will be displayed under 'Sharing' in the details view of the file or folder.

■ **Public** A public link lets anyone view, but not edit, the files and folders you share online. Public links also make it possible for anyone to search and find your publicly shared files. This is a convenient way to share files with lots of people, but it's important to make sure that you only create public links to files and folders that you do want people to find easily online.

Help! Someone has edited my files on SkyDrive

If you want to stop a particular person from making changes to your files, you need to change the permission settings for that person.

1 Sign on to SkyDrive.

2 Click the shared file or folder that has been edited and expand the rightmost pane if it's collapsed.

3 Under 'Sharing', you will see a list of people with their permission settings. Click the **drop-down arrow** for the person whose permissions you'd like to change and select either **Can view** or **Can edit**. People with **Can view** permission can only view files, but not change them. People with **Can edit** permission can view and edit files.

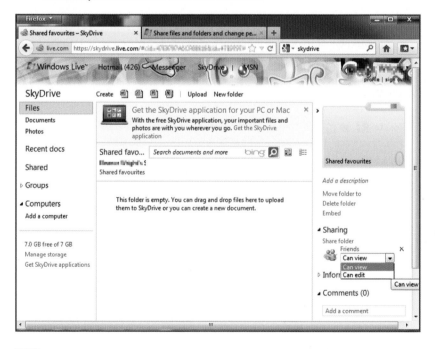

4 Your changes will be saved automatically.

5 To remove someone from the list of people with permissions to a file or folder, click the **small cross** next to their name or group name to 'Remove permissions'. Your changes will be saved automatically.

Online storage: Dropbox

Dropbox is a free service that offers online storage and file synchronisation. Once signed up to an account with Dropbox, you create a special folder on your computer, which Dropbox then synchronises with a folder on its own servers. This means you can access the same folder and its contents regardless of the computer or device used. Like SkyDrive, it's a useful way to store and share photos, video and documents between computers and other devices.

Some of my files refuse to sync from my Windows PC to a Mac

First check to see if both computers are connected to the internet and are signed into the same Dropbox account. If certain files then don't appear, the file itself may have an issue that prevents you from seeing it as expected on a specific operating system.

> ### Jargon buster
> **Metadata** Information stored within a digital file. Most digital cameras store photos with extra information - known as metadata - and includes information such as copyright details or creation date.

To ensure your files and folders sync correctly on other operating systems, try to follow these guidelines:

- Don't use file names that have characters that aren't compatible with Windows (see page 120).
- Files and folders can't have more than 260 characters in their name. Shorten them to ensure they sync properly.
- Be careful with your use of upper and lower case characters. Most operating systems won't differentiate file or folder names by case. So, for example, if you have a folder named 'Holiday photos' and one named 'holiday photos', Dropbox will sync both folders, but on Windows one will appear as a copy of the original file.
- Avoid ending file and folder names with full stops as these won't sync properly between operating systems.
- Avoid syncing files that have metadata attached, including Mac aliases or Windows shortcuts. These types of files will usually only work on the operating systems they were created on.

Internet and web problems

Help! I've deleted a file by mistake – how can I get it back?

By default Dropbox keeps snapshots of every change in your Dropbox folder over the last 30 days. So, even if you have made and saved changes to a file, or the file has been damaged or deleted, you can quickly restore the file to an older version.

1 Log onto the Dropbox website. Then click the **Show deleted files** icon on the blue action bar at the top of the window.

2 Deleted files will be shown in grey. Right click the file you want to recover.

3 From the pop-up menu, click **Restore**.

4 A window will open asking for confirmation of the action. Click **Restore**. The file will appear with its name in black in the original location.

I can't see my file in the 'Show deleted files' list

If you have clicked **Show deleted files** but the file you want to recover isn't listed, you may still be able to recover it from your Dropbox cache. Dropbox keeps a collection of your files in its cache folder for up to three days after they're moved or deleted. If you can't find your file using all other practical methods, you can try to recover the file from the Dropbox cache as a last resort.

To rescue a file from your Dropbox cache, follow these instructions:

1 Open a new 'Windows Explorer' window by clicking on the **Start** menu and then on **My Computer**.

2 Type the following code into the location bar at the top of the window: **%HOMEPATH%\Dropbox\.dropbox.cache**, then press **return**.

3 This will show the Dropbox cache folder in your Application Data folder.

4 Locate the file and drag it out of the Dropbox cache folder into another folder on your hard drive.

I've uploaded my photos to Dropbox but I can't seem to share them

Dropbox makes it easy to store photos online – you can simply create or drag a folder full of images into your Photos folder. Then to share photos with friends and family, you need a link to that location.

1 Copy the photos you want to share to the Photos folder in your Dropbox.

2 You can create subfolders to help organise your photos in the Photos folder. To do this, right click anywhere inside the Photos folder and select **New...** and then click **Folder**.

3 Right click the folder you want to share and from the pop-up menu click **Get link**.

4 You can email your link from within Dropbox or post to Facebook or Twitter. Alternatively, copy the link from the browser address bar and copy it to your choice of email program or social networking site.

Home working

By reading this chapter you'll get to grips with:

- Fixing problems with Word
- Solving issues with Excel and PowerPoint
- Creating and working with PDFs

Word: document problems

One of the world's most used software programs, Word 2010 is a powerful word-processing tool that is suitable for writing everything from a homework essay, letter to a bank, or even a family newsletter. However, working with Word can throw up some issues from document creation to formatting text, which can prove really frustrating.

I want to set up a default folder to save my Word documents

If you hate having to navigate through the maze of folders each time you save a new Word document, you can easily configure the default Word directory to a location you use most frequently. This could be on your hard drive or even a Windows Live SkyDrive account.

1 With Word open, click the **File** tab and then click **Options**.

2 In the 'Word Options' dialog box, click **Save**.

3 In the 'Default file location' field, click **Browse...**.

4 Select the folder you would like to use as the default save location for Word, such as My Documents.

5 Click **OK** and **OK** again to save your changes.

I've created a new template and need some text

When you're creating a new template for a Word document, it can be useful to include some text to experiment with in order to decide layout and formatting options. However, there's no need to type reams of random characters on the page, instead use Word's random text feature. Type **=rand( )** on the page and hit **Enter** on the keyboard to yield a paragraph of text. If you prefer to use the standard lorem ipsum text instead, type **=lorem( )** to generate a paragraph.

To generate more than one paragraph of random or lorem ipsum text, insert a number that represents the number of paragraphs required between the two brackets, so typing **=lorem(8)** will generate eight paragraphs of lorem ipsum.

Jargon buster

Lorem ipsum A piece of garbled Latin text that's commonly used as mock-content when creating or testing a template, page layout or font usage.

Why can't I collapse the Navigation pane's expanded view?

Word's Navigation pane makes working with long documents very easy. Not only does it let you scroll quickly through a list or page view of your document, you can reorganise the document by dragging section headings to new positions or insert or delete sections. To open the Navigation pane, on the **View** tab, in the 'Show' group, select the **Navigation Pane** check box.

The Navigation pane will open on the left of your document showing a fully expanded view of the document. If your document is particularly long with multiple nested headings, you may find it easier to view if it is collapsed to just the main headings.

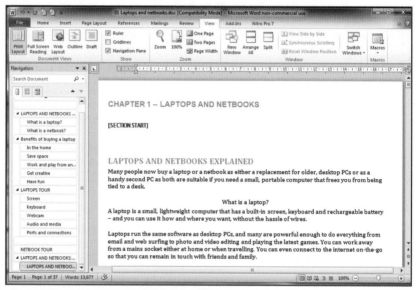

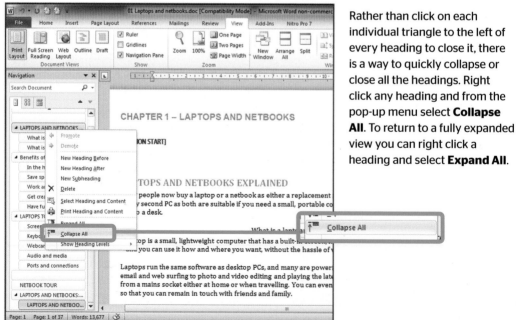

Rather than click on each individual triangle to the left of every heading to close it, there is a way to quickly collapse or close all the headings. Right click any heading and from the pop-up menu select **Collapse All**. To return to a fully expanded view you can right click a heading and select **Expand All**.

Someone changed my document without switching on tracking changes

If someone else reviews and makes changes to your document without first selecting track changes, you can use Word's 'Compare' feature to look at two versions of the same document at once to try to identify the changes.

1 With Word open, on the **Review** tab, click **Compare** and from the drop-down menu click **Compare...**.

2 Select the 'Original document' and then the 'Revised document' by using the drop-down menus beside each or clicking on the **Folder** icons beside each box to browse for documents on your computer.

3 Click **More>>** to view other settings that you want to compare in the two documents.

4 Under 'Comparison settings', tick the check boxes for the elements you want to compare between files.

5 Under 'Show changes', select the options you want and click **OK**.

6 Word will open a window showing a new document with the revised text of your document highlighting the changes made. Alongside will be the original and revised versions. You can accept or reject changes here and save the new document as a separate file – the source documents remain unchanged.

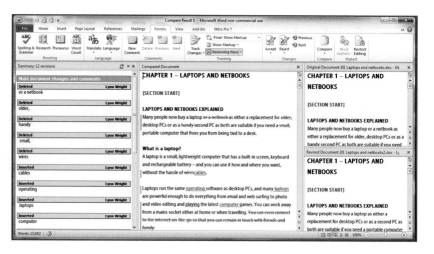

I've forgotten to remove tracked changes before saving a document

If you have used tracked changes in your document, but forgotten to remove them before you send the file to someone else, they'll be easily viewable to anyone who then turns on the option to display revisions and changes.

Word has an option that warns you whenever you try to save or print a document that contains revision information. It also warns you if you try to email it from Word's menus. However, you must turn on this warning in advance:

1 Click the **File** tab and click **Options**.

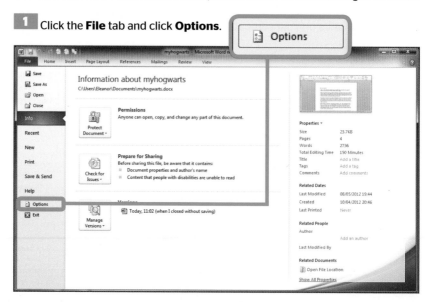

2 Click **Trust Center**.

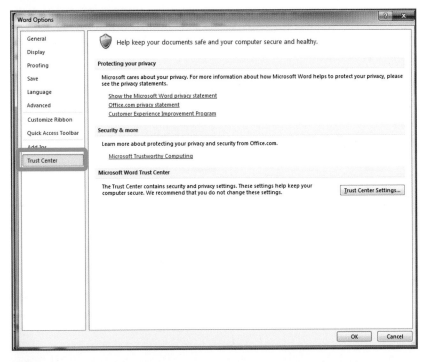

3 Click on **Trust Center Settings...**, and then click **Privacy Options**.

4 Add a check mark next to 'Warn before printing, saving or sending a file that contains tracked changes or comments'.

Word: formatting problems

Word offers lots of ways to format a document, from changing text and altering layouts to adding tables and working with graphics. In fact, there are so many formatting tools and detailed options, that it can be a challenge to find and use them to good effect.

I want to use page numbers but not on the title page

It's easy to set up page numbers in Word, but by default every page of your document will be numbered including title pages. However, there's a quick way to skip numbering on a title page.

1 On the **Insert** tab, in 'Header & Footer', click **Footer** and then select the type of page numbering you want.

2 When you have placed the footer on the page you will see a new **Design** tab on the Ribbon under 'Header & Footer Tools'. On this tab, in the 'Options' group, tick the check box next to 'Different First Page'.

I can't tell what styles are used in a document

To see what styles a document contains, activate the Style Area Pane, which can be seen in Word's 'Draft' and 'Outline' views.

1 Click the **File** tab and then click **Options**.

2 Click **Advanced**.

3 Under 'Display', set the width of the 'Style area pane width in Draft and Outline views' to 2.5cm (1 inch)

4 Click **OK**.

5 On the **View** tab, in 'Document Views', select either **Draft** or **Outline** view. Both views will show a column to the left of your text that details the style for each paragraph.

6 To remove the Style Area Pane, click and drag the vertical black line all the way to the left.

My paragraph style has changed unexpectedly

First check to see if automatic updating is turned on for the style. If it is, any changes you make to a paragraph that has the style applied to it are automatically saved in the style itself. This means that the formatting of all other paragraphs in the document that use the same style will automatically update to match the altered paragraph.

Bear in mind that if your style is based on another style that has changed, it will also be affected. To turn off automatic updating:

1 On the **Home** tab, in the 'Styles' group, right click the name of the style.

2 From menu that then pops up, click **Modify...**.

3 In the 'Modify Style' dialog box, clear the 'Automatically update' check box to disable automatic updating of the style.

4 Click **OK**.

5 If your style is based on another and you don't want it to change when you alter the base style, you can change it in the 'Modify Style' dialog box. Follow Steps 1 and 2 and in the 'Style based on' box select **(no style)** and then click **OK**.

Help, my table keeps breaking across two pages

To avoid a table being split across pages use the following steps:

1 Right click the table and from the pop-up menu click **Properties**.

2 Click the **Row** tab.

3 Click to select the 'Allow row to break across pages' check box and untick it.

4 Click **OK**.

I would like to fit text onto one page. Can I do this?

When the text in your document spills over onto another page by a lone sentence or two, Word's handy 'Shrink to Fit' command can help. It reduces the font size of the text so that it fits on one less page than it used to. It works best with only a few lines of text running over, otherwise the font size may be too small to read.

The only problem is that this command is hidden in Word. To use it, you have to add it to either the Ribbon or the Quick Access Toolbar. Here's how to add it to the Quick Access Toolbar:

1 Right click the **Quick Access Toolbar** at the top of the window and select **Customize Quick Access Toolbar...**.

2 In the 'Word Options' dialog box, the list box on the right shows the commands that are currently on the Quick Access Toolbar. The list box on the left shows the commands you can add. Click the 'Choose Commands from' **drop-down arrow** and select **All Commands** to see a full list of the commands available.

3 Scroll through the list and click on **Shrink One Page**.

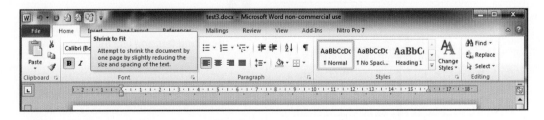

4 Click the **Add>>** button that sits between the two boxes. The command will be added to the Quick Access Toolbar.

5 Click **OK** to exit the dialog box. The 'Shrink to Fit' command will now be on the Quick Access Toolbar.

I've typed lots of text without realising my caps lock was on

If you have been typing away happily but, when you look up at the screen, realise that you have hit the Caps Lock button by accident at some point, your text will be in the wrong case (see jargon buster, opposite).

There's no need to delete and retype this text. Word has a quick way to correct it. Simply highlight the text you need to correct and on the **Home** tab, in the 'Font' group, click the button with a Capital A and a small A next to each other (Aa). From the drop-down menu, select **tOGGLE cASE**. Your text should now have the correct mix of character case.

I need to use symbols that aren't on my keyboard

When working on a document, you may need to use a special character, such as the copyright symbol, or you may need to type the temperature in degrees or add an acute accent to a French word. Fortunately with Word you're not limited to just the characters on your keyboard – you can choose from a wide range of foreign language letters or symbols. To insert a symbol or special character into your text:

1 Place your cursor in the text where you want the symbol or special character to appear.

2 On the **Insert** tab, in the 'Symbol' group, click **Symbol**.

3 From the drop-down menu, click a symbol to insert it directly into your text.

4 If the symbol or character you want isn't on the list, open the 'Symbol' dialog box by clicking **More Symbols...** from the menu.

5 Here you have lots of options. For example, you can select from symbols or characters and use the Subset drop-down list to see even more options or select a decorative font, such as Wingdings, from the Font menu to see unusual characters. Some symbols have shortcut keys – these are shown at the bottom of the 'Symbol' dialog box.

6 Click **Insert** to insert the character or symbol in your text and close the 'Symbol' dialog box.

Subset: Currency Symbols

Word keeps changing my text to something I didn't type

Unexpected changes to your text are usually the result of Word's 'AutoFormat As You Type' and 'AutoCorrect' functions. Both are very useful but if you don't understand what they're doing, it can be frustrating. Switched on by default, these features correct common typing mistakes and format your text automatically based on a predefined list of options. AutoFormat may, for example, automatically turn all website and email address into hyperlinks, replace hyphens with dashes, and single quote marks with proper curly quote marks. It's a good idea to look at the options in Word's 'AutoCorrect Options' and choose the ones you actually want.

1 With Word open, click the **File** tab and in the left-hand pane click **Options**.

2 Click **Proofing**, and then click the **AutoCorrect Options...** button.

3 Click the **AutoFormat As You Type** tab.

4 Select or clear the check boxes for the options that you want to enable or disable under 'Replace as you type', 'Apply as you type' and 'Automatically as you type'. After you do this, you can format these items manually. To effectively turn off Word's autoformatting, clear all the check boxes.

5 Click **OK** twice.

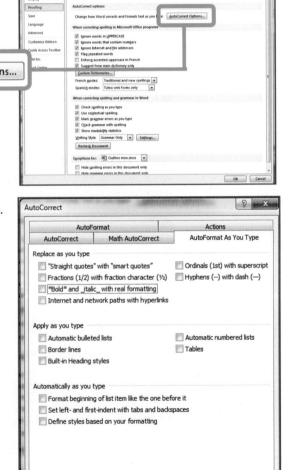

Jargon buster
Upper and lower case Describes the appearance of letters. Text is in upper case when all capital letters are used (for example UPPER CASE) and when no capitals letters are used, type has been set in lower case (for example lower case).

Excel: problems with formulas

The world's most popular spreadsheet program, Excel 2010 lets you store, organise and analyse information, create budgets and reports, manage inventories, produce planners and calendars, and much more. Stuffed full of powerful features, getting the most from Excel can involve a steep learning curve but knowing how to deal with common problems including creating formulas, saving and printing can help speed you on your way.

I keep getting error messages in my formulas

If, when building a formula, you make a mistake, Excel may return an incorrect result such as #VALUE! You can avoid problems by remembering the following rules for creating a formula:

- A formula must start with the equal sign (=).
- Don't add a space before the equal sign (=).
- Make sure your data is in the correct format; for example, numbers rather than text.
- Make sure you select the correct data range.

Excel uses standard mathematical operators in its equations. The most-used ones are:

- A plus sign for addition (+).
- A minus sign for subtraction (-).
- An asterisk for multiplication (*).
- A forward slash for division (/).

Order of operations

When working with complex formulas, Excel performs a calculation based on the following standard order of operations:

1 Parentheses.

2 Exponents (to the power of).

3 Multiplication and division, whichever comes first.

4 Addition and subtraction, whichever comes first.

Working with functions

Inserting a function into a formula also has to be done in a certain way for the function to work correctly. Here is an example to show how it works using:

=SUM(B2:B6)

First you must insert an **equal sign (=)**, then a **function name** (in this example **SUM**, which will add up the numbers in a range of cells), and then an **argument** – the information you want the formula to calculate, such as a range of cell references as shown here by **B2:B6**.

Arguments must be enclosed in **parentheses** (brackets), with individual values or cell references inside the parentheses separated by either colons or commas:

- **Colons** create a reference to a range of cells so, for example, **=AVG(D2:D15)** calculates the average of the cells from D2 through to D15.
- **Commas** separate individual values, cell references and cell ranges in the parentheses. If you use more than one argument, you must separate each with a comma. For example, **=COUNT(B2:B10,B12:B22,B26)** will count all the cell values in the three cell ranges.

Common error messages

#NAME? This happens when Excel does not recognise text in a formula. You have either entered an incorrect function name, or range name or cell reference. Check that the named cell range exists and that it's not misspelt in the formula.

#VALUE! If Excel can't determine which item of a range you want to use in your formula or if you use text instead of a number, you will see this error. For example, =D2*D3 would give this error if either cell contained text.

#REF! This error message will appear if a cell reference in a formula has been deleted or a formula has been moved to another cell and the cell references are incorrect. For example, if your formula is A2+A3 and you later delete row 3, you will get this error message. You must correct the cell references for formulas that have been copied or moved.

#DIV/0! This occurs if you try to divide a number by zero or by an empty cell. For example, if you type **=30/0** or **=E2/G3** and G3 contains a zero or is empty, you will see this error message.

#NUM! This occurs when there's a problem with a number in a formula or function. For example, it can be caused by a calculation that delivers a number too high or too small for Excel to cope with. This can also occur if the wrong data type is used in a function, which requires numerical data.

#NULL! This error message pops up when cell references are not correctly separated in the formula. For example, you forget to use a colon when typing in a cell range, so type **B2G24** instead of B2:G24. Or you have used a space rather than a mathematical operator to separate cell references in a formula.

This error message occurs when the column is too narrow to display the result of the calculation. Rather than showing an abbreviated, potentially confusing result, Excel doesn't show the answer unless there's enough space. To solve the problem, you need to autofit the column size or manually resize it.

I want to see the formulas used in all my worksheet cells, but I can only see the results

To see the formulas used in each cell you need to switch from Excel's normal display, which shows the results of the formulas in the spreadsheet, to a display mode that shows the actual formulas:

1 Click the **File** menu, and then click **Options**.

2 Click **Advanced**.

3 Scroll down the dialog box and under 'Display Options for this worksheet' add a check mark to the box next to 'Show formulas in cells instead of their calculated results'.

4 To display results again uncheck this box.

Tip

Here's a quick way to see the results of Excel's most commonly used calculations: average, count and sum. Click and select two or more cells that contain numbers, then look at the status bar at the foot of the window. Excel displays the average of the numbers, a count of the cells, and the sum. You can also use this trick with non-adjacent cells by holding down the **Ctrl key** and click on each cell you wish to select. The average, count and sum in the status bar will updated each time you click a cell.

Tip

You can toggle between these two views by simply pressing **Ctrl + `** (grave accent). Press once for Excel to display formulas instead of results. Press it again, and the results appear again. As a bonus when you select a cell with a formula, Excel outlines the cells that are referenced in the formula.

Excel: problems with saving

If you're saving an Excel workbook as an .xls file so that it can be opened in earlier versions of Excel, it's a good idea to run the Compatibility Checker. This checks for potential compatibility issues such as a significant loss of functionality and suggest ways to resolve the problem.

I'm saving an Excel 2010 workbook as an Excel 97-2003 file and getting a warning message

When saving an Excel 2010 workbook as an Excel 97-2003 file (.xls), the Compatibility Checker automatically scans your workbook looking for issues that will result in loss of functionality or a change in the way things look.

> Click **Find** to locate issues in the worksheet or **Fix** to resolve simple issues or for more complex issues, click **Help** for more information.

It then displays the results in a dialog box flagging potential problems, which fall into two categories: minor loss of fidelity and significant loss of functionality. The first includes such things as cell formatting that uses special effects or shadows, which are not supported in an earlier version of Excel. These will not display properly when the workbook is opened and so you have the option to remove formatting before you save.

Major problems relate to features that are not available in earlier versions of Excel. In this example, the workbook uses sparklines – a feature new to Excel. The cells containing the sparklines will appear blank when the workbook is opened in an earlier version of Excel. To run the Compatibility Checker:

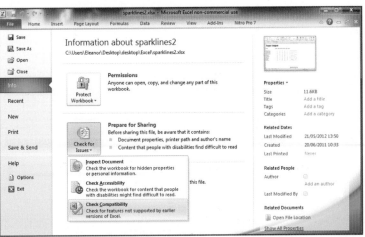

1 Click **File** and then click **Info**.

2 Click **Check for Issues**.

3 Click **Check Compatibility**.

4 The dialog box that opens provides details of the features that may be lost or not work if the workbook is opened in an earlier version of Excel.

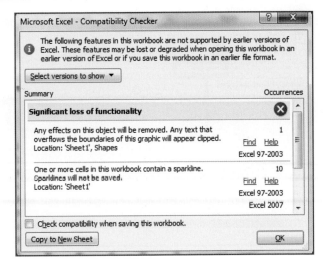

Excel: printing problems

You can preview and print your Excel worksheets using the Print pane.
To open this, click the **File** tab to see the Backstage view, then click **Print**.
The 'Print' pane appears, with the print settings on the left and a preview of
your worksheets on the right. Excel offers lots of options for printing all or
part of a worksheet but sometimes it can be frustrating trying to get your
printout the way you need it to be.

Excel only prints part of my worksheet

Check whether a print area is defined. If the worksheet contains a print
area, Excel will print only this and leave the rest blank. To see whether your
worksheet contains a print area, click **Page Break Preview** on the 'View' menu.
The area of the worksheet that appears with a light coloured background is the
area that's printed. The non-printing area will look grey.

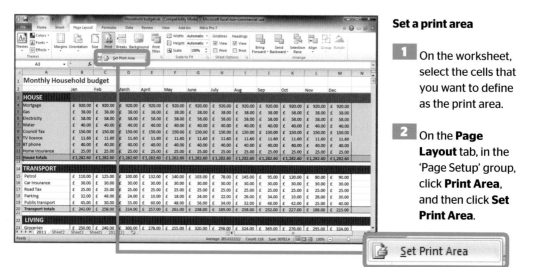

Set a print area

1 On the worksheet,
select the cells that
you want to define
as the print area.

2 On the **Page
Layout** tab, in the
'Page Setup' group,
click **Print Area**,
and then click **Set
Print Area**.

> Set Print Area

Clear a print area

1 Click anywhere on the worksheet.

2 On the **Page
Layout** tab, in
the 'Page Setup'
group, click **Clear
Print Area**.

> Clear Print Area

When I print, Excel adds extra rows to my worksheet

If you select an entire row or column before applying formatting, Excel formats all empty cells out to the bottom row or last column. It then stores the formatting information for all cells, resulting in large files and cells that print regardless of being empty. To fix this problem, do one of the following:

1 If you don't want to start a new worksheet, press **F5**, click **Special...** in the 'Go To' dialog box, and then click **Last cell**. Delete all the rows up to your actual data and then save the workbook.

2 Insert a blank worksheet. On the original worksheet, select only the cells that you want to print and copy them to the new blank worksheet.

When I print my worksheet it breaks across two pages

You can prevent columns or rows from spilling over the edge of a page by shrinking the sheet so that it is one page wide or tall.

1 Click **File** and then click **Print**.

2 Click **Page Setup**.

3 In the 'Page Setup' dialog box, on the **Page** tab and under 'Scaling', click **Fit to**. Then do one of the following:

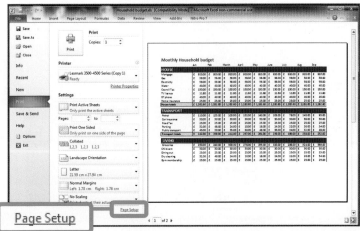

To print to fit a paper width:
- ▬ In the first box beside **Fit to**, enter **1** (for 1 page wide).
- ▬ In the second box, delete the value so that the number of pages tall is unspecified.

To print a worksheet on a specific number of pages:
- ▬ In the boxes beside **Fit to**, enter the number of pages on which you want to print the work.

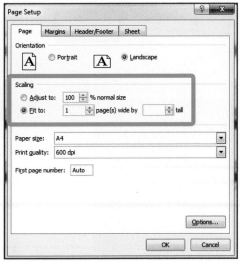

PowerPoint: presentation creation problems

Part of Microsoft Office, PowerPoint 2010 is software that uses slides to create a presentation. Along with text and charts, you can add images, video and animation to slides but sometimes successfully incorporating media files can be troublesome.

I can't get the music to stop after a certain number of slides

Many people try trimming an audio track so that it plays across a certain number of slides and then stops. However, this approach may not always work – often the trim is ignored and the whole sound file plays. Here's how to stop your music after a specified number of slides:

1 On the **Insert** tab, click the **Audio** drop-down arrow and select **Audio From File...**.

2 Select an audio file and click **Insert** in the first slide where you want it to begin.

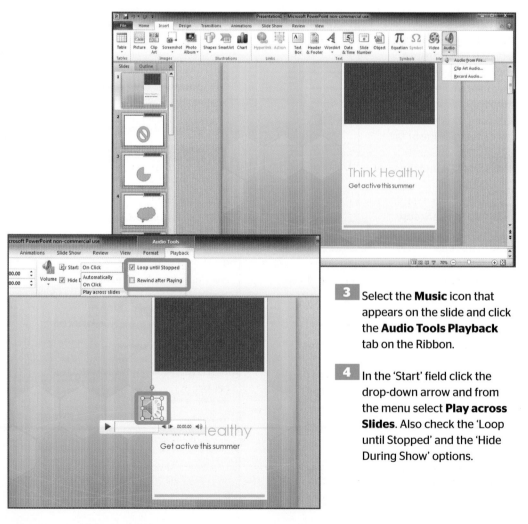

3 Select the **Music** icon that appears on the slide and click the **Audio Tools Playback** tab on the Ribbon.

4 In the 'Start' field click the drop-down arrow and from the menu select **Play across Slides**. Also check the 'Loop until Stopped' and the 'Hide During Show' options.

5 On the Ribbon, click the **Animations** tab.

6 With the music icon still selected, click the small arrow at the bottom right of the 'Animations' group to launch the 'Play Audio' dialog box.

7 In the **Effect** tab, in the 'After' option, change the value from 999 to the number of slides after which you want the music to stop.

The music in my presentation won't play when it's viewed on another computer

One of the most common problems with PowerPoint involves music not playing once you've emailed a presentation to someone else. PowerPoint offers two choices for including audio in a presentation: linking and embedding.

If you embed an audio file it becomes part of the actual PowerPoint presentation file. Embedding audio (or video) files will guarantee their playback regardless of which computer the presentation is played on, but it also makes the presentation file significantly larger.

When you link a file, you essentially tell PowerPoint where to find the file on your hard disk so it can play it when necessary – the file itself remains separate to the PowerPoint presentation. Linking audio helps keep your presentation's file size down, but when you transfer the presentation to another computer you must transfer the audio files as well and update the links on the new computer or device otherwise the links are severed and the audio won't play as expected.

While the answer to this problem may seem straightforward – simply embed the audio files in your presentation – the reality is a little more complicated. Despite the popularity of audio formats such as MP3, the only audio files that can be embedded into PowerPoint are those in the WAV file format. The downside to this solution, however, is that WAV files tend to be huge, thus making the presentation far too large to email or upload to an online sharing site.

Furthermore, if you've used lots of WAV audio files in your presentation, you may need a powerful up-to-date computer to be able to successfully open or play the presentation.

Jargon buster

WAV Sometimes written as WAVE, WAV is short for Waveform Audio File Format as used by Windows audio files. WAV sound files end with .wav and can be played by nearly all Windows applications that support sound.

However, there's a way that you can fool PowerPoint into thinking that an MP3 file is really a WAV file and so embed it in your presentation. You need to first download a free piece of software called CDex (http://cdexos.sourceforge.net/). Here's how:

1 In CDex, click **Convert** and from the drop-down menu click **Add RIFF-WAV(s) header to MP2 or MP3 file(s)**.

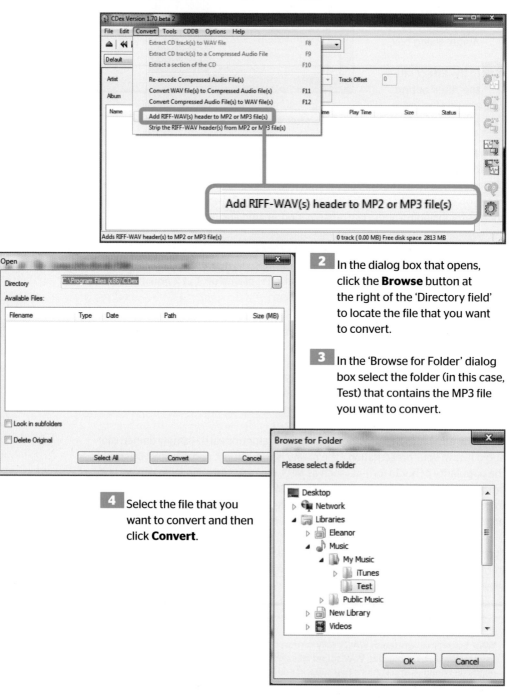

2 In the dialog box that opens, click the **Browse** button at the right of the 'Directory field' to locate the file that you want to convert.

3 In the 'Browse for Folder' dialog box select the folder (in this case, Test) that contains the MP3 file you want to convert.

4 Select the file that you want to convert and then click **Convert**.

5 The .mp3 file is given a WAV extension, but it's still in an MP3 format despite the .wav extension at the end of the file name.

6 Close the CDex program.

7 In PowerPoint, click the **Insert** tab and click the 'Audio' **drop-down arrow**. Then click on **Audio from File....**

8 Locate the file you want to add and then click **Insert**.

The playback of video in my presentation is very slow

Video and audio playback problems range from slow performance to dropped frames or stuttering. Fortunately there are a few things you can try to improve video and audio playback when running a PowerPoint presentation.

In PowerPoint

■ Compress any audio and video files (see page 151) – particularly those that are embedded – to keep the presentation's file size as small as possible.

■ Make sure linked media files are in the same directory as the presentation so that they play correctly.

■ Avoid using special effects, such as shadows, reflections, glow effects, soft edges and rotation on your video files.

In Windows

- Ensure that your video card drivers are up to date. See page 169 for more information as to how to do this.
- Turn the hardware acceleration 'on'. To do this, click the **File** tab, under **Help**, click **Options**, click **Advanced**, and then under 'Display', clear the 'Disable hardware graphics acceleration' check box.
- Make sure that there's enough free disk space on the computer that you will deliver your presentation on.
- Exit all other programs before you run your presentation.
- Clean out your Window's TEMP folder. If there are lots of files here, it can make PowerPoint sluggish, so it's a good idea to periodically delete files in your TEMP folder. Here's how:

1 Close PowerPoint and all other programs you are using.

Run

Type the name of a program, folder, document, or Internet resource, and Windows will open it for you.

Open: %temp%

OK   Cancel   Browse...

2 Click **Start** and then type **run** in the search box.

3 Double click on the **Run** icon at the top of the window.

4 In the 'Run' dialog box, type **%temp%**.

5 Click **OK**.

6 Select the .tmp files you want to remove by clicking on each one or select all, and then press the **Delete** key on your keyboard. You can delete any file here – although you may see an 'access error' message if a file is in use. If so, you can choose to try again or cancel, or If you've selected all files to be deleted and see this message, you can skip the file in question and continuing deleting the others.

Tip

If you have used notes in your presentation, you will probably want to remove them before you share the presentation with others. Here's a quick way to remove them all in one go. With the file open, click **File** and then **Info**. Click **Check for Issues** and from the drop-down menu, click **Inspect Document**. Make sure the check box next to 'Presentation Notes' is selected, and then click **Inspect**. Click **Remove all** next to anything you don't want in your document.

Name	Date modified	Type
{03EDF1DE-50D7-4021-A24D-6E151C43CC43}	25/12/2010 11:14	File folder
{6F729A34-B418-4C4B-9B47-B39CE14DF081}	26/12/2010 13:52	File folder
{8F26B801-E497-4380-9D9E-70A9F4E04456}	26/12/2010 14:08	File folder
{17DFE37C-064E-4834-AD8F-A4B2B4DF68F8}	13/09/2011 11:15	File folder
{21CB04BC-E77F-4EEE-9DF9-AD721FD73F36}	25/12/2010 11:00	File folder
{40b57985-e0f0-4c34-8c12-b117aad0b8ad}	19/06/2010 16:04	File folder
{949092DB-4F5F-430C-A228-243C8F81A279}	26/12/2010 13:29	File folder
{DC160072-9482-4B18-B960-CFAA797E3939}	25/12/2010 11:18	File folder
{f420a2ca-00ac-4ed5-940a-1db6ccc13880}	14/06/2012 19:41	File folder
~e5.0001.dir.0000	08/06/2012 14:50	File folder
3784.dir	06/03/2012 14:13	File folder
04130605-00001028-mvuv3nm5wk	13/04/2012 06:05	File folder
04131406-00001030-5txd6ygcch	13/04/2012 14:06	File folder
06221337-00000c88-je7k7z2364	22/06/2011 13:37	File folder
06291320-000017fc-a6wc7gdzoq	29/06/2012 13:50	File folder
06291320-0000075c-c9puf8v9lb	29/06/2012 13:20	File folder
08081801-00000e94-09w57z16fv	08/08/2011 18:01	File folder
061914440000149c81qru6l2hi	19/06/2010 14:44	File folder
061914440000149cbtgebg3ky4	19/06/2010 14:44	File folder
061914440000149cc14mxj48xp	19/06/2010 14:44	File folder
061914440000149czwmyj5fqss	19/06/2010 14:44	File folder
061914450000149c4pg8r70lzq	19/06/2010 14:45	File folder
061914450000149c6t6iyz614wj	19/06/2010 14:45	File folder
061914450000149cgsd4l6sg9o	19/06/2010 14:45	File folder
061914460000149co5xrjevykx	19/06/2010 14:46	File folder

2,751 items

PowerPoint: sharing presentation problems

Having created a presentation in PowerPoint, you'll want to share it with others either via an email, or uploading it to a website or simply presenting it on a friend's PC. However, you may encounter some common playback errors.

My PowerPoint presentation is too large to send as an email attachment

Adding lots of images to your PowerPoint presentation can result in a very large file size, which makes emailing the finished file to others difficult.

Ensure that the images you add to your presentation are in a compressed graphics file formats such as .jpg or .gif, and if possible, optimise your photos by reducing their resolution as required and cropping unwanted areas. If, however, you have already placed all the images on your presentation, PowerPoint has features that can help you compress images and reduce file size.

> You will only see the 'Picture Tools' and 'Format' tabs once you have selected a picture. You may have to double click the picture to select it and open the 'Format' tab.

Compress a picture

1 Click the picture(s) that you want to change the resolution for.

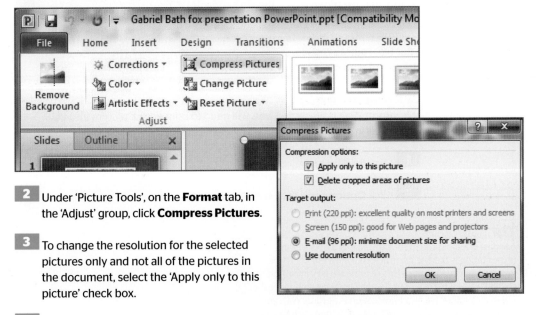

2 Under 'Picture Tools', on the **Format** tab, in the 'Adjust' group, click **Compress Pictures**.

3 To change the resolution for the selected pictures only and not all of the pictures in the document, select the 'Apply only to this picture' check box.

4 If you have cropped a picture, make sure you delete the unwanted areas in order to reduce the file size. To do this, select the 'Delete cropped areas of pictures' check box.

5 Under 'Target output', click the resolution that you want. For example, to email the presentation, select 'E-mail (96 ppi): minimize document for sharing'.

Change the default resolution for the presentation

You can also change the picture resolution for all pictures in the presentation, which by default it is set to a target of Print (220ppi).

1 Click the **File** tab.

2 Click **Options** and then click **Advanced**.

3 Under 'Image Size and Quality', click the presentation that you want to set the default picture resolution for.

4 In 'Set default target output to', click the resolution that you want. The lower the resolution the smaller the file size, although you'll lose image quality somewhat.

Delete all picture editing data

If you have edited a picture in PowerPoint, information about these changes is stored in your file. You can reduce the size of your file by deleting this editing data. However, once this information is discarded, you will need to reinsert the picture into your presentation if you want to undo any changes you have made.

> If you want the highest quality picture resolution and are happy to accept a larger file size, you can turn compression off (see Compress a picture, page 151).

1 Click the **File** tab.

2 Click **Options** and then click **Advanced**.

Tip
Another good trick to reduce the size of a PowerPoint presentation is to save it again with a different file name. PowerPoint usually stores lots of unnecessary information, such as earlier drafts and previously used images. Once it's saved as another file, this information is purged. With your presentation open, click the **File** tab and then click **Save As...** and give it another name. Then click **Save**. You should then have a second presentation that is often smaller than the original copy.

3 Under 'Image Size and Quality', click the document from which you want to remove picture-editing data.

4 Also select the 'Discard editing data' check box.

Help! The fonts in my presentation change when played on another PC

Unless you intend to run a presentation only on your own computer, you need to embed your fonts to avoid font overrides from the host computer. To do this:

1 Click the **File** tab.

2 Click **Options** and then click **Save**.

3 Then check 'Embed fonts in the file'.

Can my presentation be viewed on a PC that doesn't have PowerPoint

Even if you haven't PowerPoint installed on your computer, you can still open and view PowerPoint presentations by using PowerPoint Viewer. This is a free download from Microsoft's website. Once PowerPoint Viewer is downloaded and installed, your friend will be able to open, view and print presentations, but not edit them.

Working with PDFs

Created by Adobe, a Portable Document Format or PDF is the most popular file format for sharing digital information. A PDF file can be opened on any type of computer or device using Adobe's free Adobe Reader software – no matter what software was originally used to create the file. Furthermore, a PDF file accurately preserves the look and feel of the original document complete with fonts, colours, images and layout.

Nothing happens when I try to open a PDF on my desktop

Before you can open a PDF file, you need make sure you have the correct software to read the file.

1 Click **Start** and type **Adobe Reader** in the search box. If it appears in the list, double click to open. If it is not already installed on your computer, type the following address into your web browser: **http://get.adobe.com/uk/reader/**.

2 Click **Download now**, and follow the on-screen instructions to download and install the software.

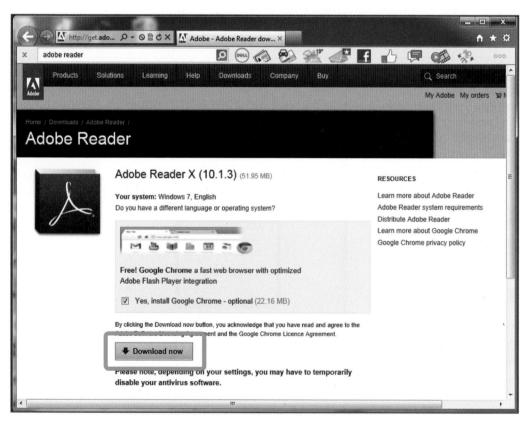

3 Once the software is installed, it should automatically open any .pdf file that you double click on with your mouse.

My web browser shows a blank page when I try to open a PDF

When you click on a PDF file online it will either open directly within your web browser window or open in a separate window. However, if you see a blank page, red X icon or error page, it could be for one of the following reasons:

■ The web browser isn't configured correctly or is not PDF-capable.
■ The web server on which the PDF file is stored isn't working properly.
■ Adobe Reader can't read the PDF file.

To fix the problem try the following steps:

1 Restart your computer and try opening the PDF again. This often resolves common problems.

2 Check your web browser can open PDF files by dragging a previously saved PDF file from your hard disk onto your web browser window. If Adobe Reader displays the file but not in the web browser, the web server has a problem serving the PDF file. Contact the website from which you downloaded the PDF file that you can't open.

3 Try opening a PDF from a different website. If you're able to view other PDFs, then the problem lies with the PDF itself or the web server. In which case, contact the website.

4 Check you have the latest version of Adobe Reader installed (see opposite).

5 If you're using Internet Explorer or Firefox try deleting temporary internet files. To do this:

■ **Internet Explorer** Click the **Tools** icon (it looks like a cog) on the top right of the window, and then click **Internet Options**. In the 'Browsing history' area of the **General** tab, click **Delete....** Select 'Temporary Internet files' and deselect all other options. Then click **Delete**. Click **OK** to close 'Internet Options'. Try to open the PDF again from the website.

■ **Firefox** Click **Firefox** in the top left corner and then **Options**. Under the **Privacy** tab, click **clear your recent history**. In the next dialog box deselect all the options except 'Cache'. (If you can't see the options, click the **Details** button.) Click **Clear Now**. Then try to open the PDF again from the website.

I'm trying to open a PDF but it's asking me for a password
When creating a PDF, you can add a password to a PDF to prevent unauthorised users from viewing the document. To open a PDF with this level of security, you must enter the password when prompted. If the person who created the PDF has not shared the password with you, you cannot open the PDF.

I don't want to buy special software to create a PDF
There's no need to buy Adobe's Acrobat PDF creation software if you're using Microsoft Office 2010. Office comes with a built-in PDF writer so you can create PDFs in Word (as shown below), Excel and PowerPoint with a few clicks.

1 With the Word document open, click the **File** tab to go to the Backstage view.

2 Click **Save As**.

3 If necessary, enter a name for the file in the File Name box.

4 In the 'Save as' type list, click **PDF** (*.pdf).

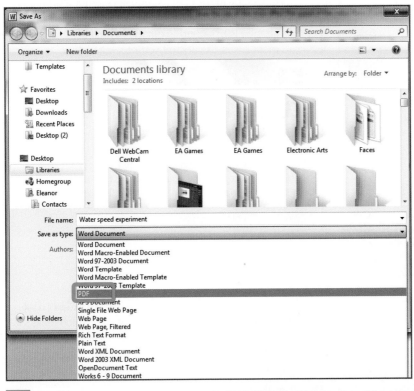

5 When you choose the PDF file type, the following options become available:

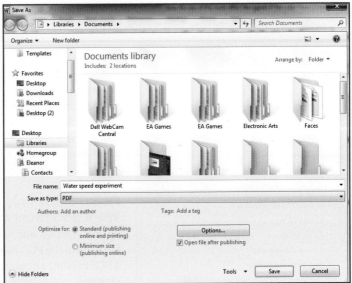

■ 'Optimize for' affects the file size and quality of the PDF that is created. If you want the smallest file size possible, perhaps for emailing the PDF to someone to read onscreen, choose 'Minimum size (publishing online)'. If, at some point, you may want a high-quality print of the PDF choose 'Standard (publishing online and printing)'.

■ 'Open file after publishing': tick this box, if you want to view the document as a PDF after saving.

Options

Page range
- ◉ All
- ○ Current page
- ○ Selection
- ○ Page(s) From: [1] To: [1]

Publish what
- ◉ Document
- ○ Document showing markup

Include non-printing information
- ☐ Create bookmarks using:
  - ◉ Headings
  - ○ Word bookmarks
- ☑ Document properties
- ☑ Document structure tags for accessibility

PDF options
- ☐ ISO 19005-1 compliant (PDF/A)
- ☑ Bitmap text when fonts may not be embedded
- ☐ Encrypt the document with a password

[OK] [Cancel]

6 Click **Options** to set what pages of the document to include in the PDF, to choose whether markup (comments) should be printed, and, if required, to change PDF settings from the default settings. In most cases, the default settings will be fine.

7 Click **OK** when finished.

8 Click **Save**.

Tip
If you're working with an application that doesn't have the ability to create PDF files, you can access the Adobe CreatePDF service at www.acrobat.com from within Reader X. This lets you convert up to five files for free and has monthly and annual plans available to purchase for this purpose.

I've created a PDF but when printed my photos look terrible

One of the best things about a PDF is that it has a small file size, which makes it a popular choice for sending files by email. The reason for this is that, while PDF keeps the exact layout and content of the original document, the information – particularly graphic elements such as photographs – is highly compressed.

When you're saving a document as a PDF, you can select a setting for optimising the file (see Step 5, page 157).

Options

Page range
- ○ All
- ○ Current page
- ○ Selection
- ◉ Page(s) From: [2] To: [6]

Publish what
- ◉ Document
- ○ Document showing markup

Include non-printing information
- ☐ Create bookmarks using:
  - ◉ Headings
  - ○ Word bookmarks
- ☑ Document properties
- ☑ Document structure tags for accessibility

PDF options
- ☐ ISO 19005-1 compliant (PDF/A)
- ☑ Bitmap text when fonts may not be embedded
- ☐ Encrypt the document with a password

[OK] [Cancel]

A smaller size PDF will have slightly poorer quality images, as they'll have been highly compressed to create a small file. This won't matter if you intend to view the PDF on screen but if you print it, the images in particularly may look poor quality. If you're unsure about which 'Optimize for' setting to choose, create a PDF in each option, then compare the two for their image quality and file size.

I want to use only a few pages from my Word document as a PDF

You can specify which pages of your document are used in the PDF. Follow the steps for creating a PDF in Word on pages 156–8 and, at Step 6, click **Options**. In the 'Options' dialog box, under 'Page range', click **All**, **Current page**, **Selection** or **Page(s)**. If you click **Page(s)**, enter the page number of the pages you wish to use.

Photos, music and video

By reading this chapter you'll get to grips with:

- Troubleshooting importing, editing and sharing photos
- Solving audio, video-editing and playback problems
- Importing and managing your music in iTunes

Problems with photos

Digital cameras have made taking photos a snap and most of us have hundreds, if not thousands, of photos filling up our computer hard drive. There are a couple of ways to import, view and edit your photos in Windows 7 and understanding some of the basics of digital photography can help you avoid common problems when working with photos.

I don't understand the difference between Windows Photo Viewer and Windows Live Photo Gallery

Many people find these similarly named programs confusing. Both are free – Windows Photo Viewer comes pre-installed with Windows 7 while Windows Live Photo Gallery is part of Windows Live Essentials, which can be downloaded from Microsoft's website.

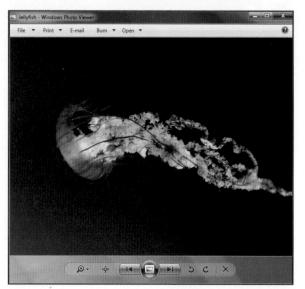

■ **Windows Photo Viewer** is used to view, print or burn digital photos onto a CD or DVD. You can also use it to attach photos to an email message. Select Windows Photo Viewer by right clicking a photo, then click **Open with...** and choose Windows Photo Viewer from the pop-up menu.

■ **Windows Live Photo Gallery** is used for all these tasks too, but more importantly offers the ability to edit photos and easily share them in a variety of ways, including uploading to Facebook and SkyDrive. Windows Live Photo Gallery is found by clicking **Start**, then clicking **All programs** and choosing it from the list of programs.

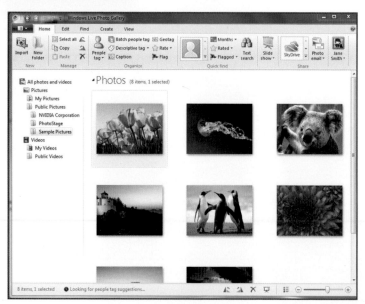

My photo is too big to email. What can I do?

If your digital camera is taking photos using high-quality or fine settings, the resulting photo files can often be too big to sensibly share with friends and family using email, but resizing can be done quickly. Windows Live Photo Gallery lets you resize a photo and automatically attaches it to an email by launching Windows Live Mail.

1 Click **Start**, then click **All Programs** and click **Windows Live Photo Gallery** from the list that appears.

2 Select the photo you want to email.

3 Click **Email** at the top of the window.

4 In the dialog box that appears, choose a size. If the recipient will only be looking at the photo onscreen, the smaller size is fine. This will be suitable for printing photos at 10 x 15cm (4 x 6in). Both medium and large are suitable for printing photos sized 12 x 18cm (5 x 7in).

5 You will see the estimated size of your attachment. Anything less than 1MB will be quick to email.

6 Click **Attach**. Windows Live Mail will launch opening a new email message with the photo already attached.

Preparing files

Photo size: Smaller: 640 x 480

Total estimated size: 90.0 KB

Attach   Cancel

My photos are taking up too much disk space

Using photo-editing software you can change the size of your photo. Making the dimensions of a photo smaller results in a smaller file size, which means you can store more photos on, say, a pen drive or display more on a digital photo frame.

Windows Live Photo Gallery lets you resize a photo to various set dimensions or to a custom size. It resizes using high-quality bicubic interpolation and all files are saved as .jpgs.

1 Click **Start**, then **All Programs** and then click **Windows Live Photo Gallery** to launch it.

2 Right click the photo you want to change and from the pop-up menu choose **Resize...**.

3 Click the 'Select a size' field **drop-down arrow** and from the drop-down menu choose a size. To set your own size, click **Custom** and then type a size into the 'Maximum dimensions' box. The dimension refers to the longest side of the photo. Photos are downsized only – if the specified dimension is larger than the longest side of the original photo, it will not be resized.

4 Click **Browse...** to choose a destination folder in which to save the newly resized photo.

5 Click **Resize and Save** to save the smaller photo.

My photos show the wrong date and time when I import them into Windows

When you take a photo, your digital camera records the date and time that it was taken and when you import your photos into the computer, this information is stored with each photo. Sometimes, however, if the camera has been set to the wrong date and time, this information won't be accurate. The good news is that you can change the date and time information on your computer.

1 Click **Start**, then click **Pictures** to open the 'Pictures library'.

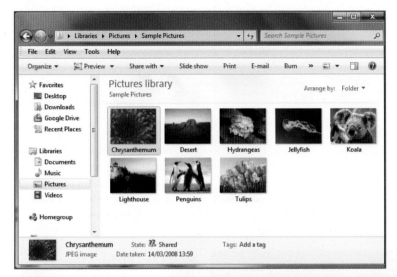

2 Select the photo or photos that you want to change. To select more than one, hold down the **Ctrl** key as you click until you have.

3 In the details pane at the bottom of the window, click next to 'Date taken', click the **Calendar** button, and then click the correct date on the calendar.

4 Click **Save** to save your changes.

Tip

If you don't see the details pane at the bottom of the Picture Library window, click **Organize**, point to 'Layout', and then click **Details pane**.

I can't print thumbnails of my photos

If you have lots of photos, it makes sense to be able to print a sheet that shows tiny versions of all your photos to help you select photos to subsequently print at full size. Viewing your photos as thumbnails makes it easier to scan a collection of photos at a glance, but it isn't obvious how to do this. Here's a fix for printing a contact sheet of your photos:

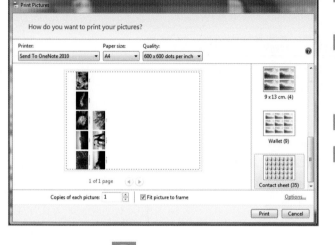

1 Click **Start**, then click **Pictures** to open the 'Pictures library'.

2 Click the photos that you want to print as thumbnails. To select more than one, hold down the **Ctrl** key as you click.

3 On the toolbar, click **Print**.

4 In the 'Print Pictures' dialog box, select the printer, paper size and type, and the number of copies you want to print, and then click **Contact sheet** in the list of print sizes.

5 Click **Print** to start printing.

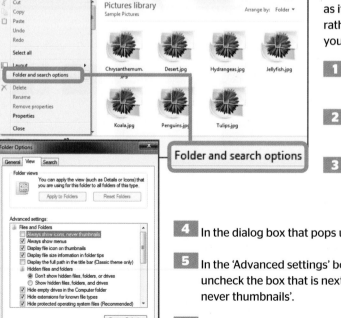

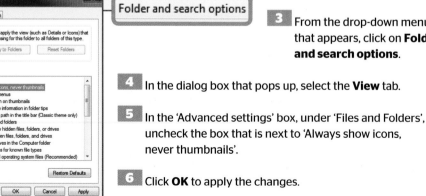

Help! My Picture library shows icons not my photos

Check your Picture folder's settings as it may be set to application icons rather than thumbnail previews of your photos.

1 Click **Start**, then click **Pictures** to open the 'Pictures library'.

2 Click **Organize** on the top-left of the menu bar.

3 From the drop-down menu that appears, click on **Folder and search options**.

4 In the dialog box that pops up, select the **View** tab.

5 In the 'Advanced settings' box, under 'Files and Folders', uncheck the box that is next to 'Always show icons, never thumbnails'.

6 Click **OK** to apply the changes.

Windows Live Photo Gallery

Part of Microsoft's free Windows Essentials suite of tools, Photo Gallery helps you organise and edit your photos, then share them online. It can be downloaded from Microsoft's website.

My Windows Live Photo Gallery won't start

If you experience problems when trying to launch Windows Live Photo Gallery, it could be the result of a corrupted database file. You can fix this by forcing Windows Live Photo Gallery to rebuild its database.

1 Click **Start** and type **run** in the search box.

2 Double click on the **Run** icon at the top of the window to open the 'Run' application.

3 In the text box, type **%userprofile%\AppData\Local\Microsoft\Windows Live Photo Gallery** and then click **OK**.

4 Check if there are any files prefixed with 'OLD_' such as 'OLD_Pictures.pd6' and delete these.

5 In the same folder, locate any files labelled 'Pictures.pd6' (or 'Pictures.pdx' where x is a number, such as 6) and add the 'OLD_' prefix to the file name to make it the same name as the file you just deleted. In this case it would then read 'OLD_Pictures.pd6'.

6 Launch Windows Photo Gallery Live and the database will be rebuilt and the program will now run successfully.

Photos, music and video

Why can't I open .gif files in Windows Live Photo Gallery?

Windows Live Photo Gallery currently doesn't support the .gif format of images, which you will often encounter on the web. If you want to open a .gif format image, Windows Live Photo Gallery will refuse to display it – luckily there's a quick fix that overcomes the problem.

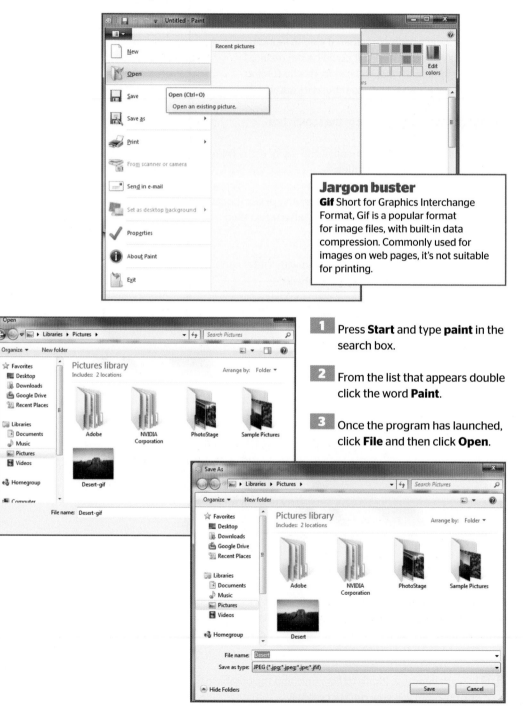

Jargon buster

Gif Short for Graphics Interchange Format, Gif is a popular format for image files, with built-in data compression. Commonly used for images on web pages, it's not suitable for printing.

1 Press **Start** and type **paint** in the search box.

2 From the list that appears double click the word **Paint**.

3 Once the program has launched, click **File** and then click **Open**.

4 Locate the .gif file that you want to open in Windows Live Photo Gallery and click **Open**.

5 Once the file has loaded, press the F12 key and then set the 'Save as type' field to **.jpg**. Click **Save** to save the file.

6 Double click the file to open it, and it should automatically open in Windows Live Photo Gallery. If it doesn't, right click the file and choose **Open with** from the pop-up menu and select **Windows Live Photo Gallery** to open the file with Windows Live Photo Gallery.

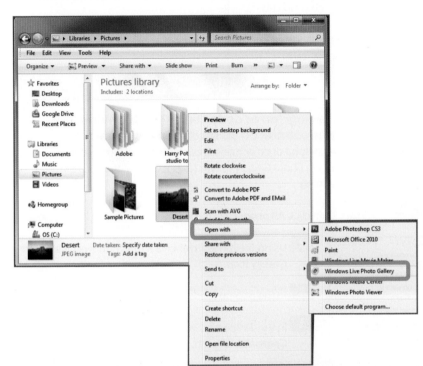

How do I stop Windows Live Photo Gallery from creating sub-folders when importing photos?

When importing photos from a camera, Windows Live Photo Gallery by default places each group of photos in a sub folder based usually on the date they were taken. If you prefer to have all your photos, for example those from a two week family holiday, placed in just one folder, you can change the default settings. Here's how:

1 Click the blue **File** tab, and from the drop-down menu click **Options**.

2 On the dialog box that appears, click the **Import** tab and then click on the 'Folder name' field – it probably reads 'Name'.

3 From the drop-down menu, click **(None)** and then click **OK**.

4 With this selected, no sub folders will be created and all photos will be imported into the folder specified in ' Import to'.

I get an error saying: 'error code:0x80070003 Windows Live Photo Gallery encountered an error and can't start'

While not the most helpful of error messages, this is a common problem when running Windows Live Photo Gallery in Windows 7. Luckily, there's a quick fix to get you up and running.

1 Click **Start**, then click **All programs** and locate Windows Live Photo Gallery.

2 Using the mouse, right click the Windows Live Photo Gallery icon.

3 In the pop-up menu that appears, select **Properties**.

4 In the 'Properties' window that appears, click the **Compatibility** tab.

5 Ensure 'Run this program in compatibility mode for:' is ticked, and choose 'Windows Vista (Service Pack 2)' from the pop-up menu. Click **Apply**, then click **OK**.

You should now be able to run Windows Live Photo Gallery successfully without getting the error code.

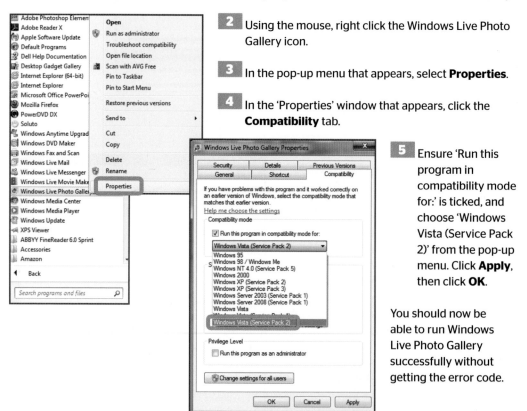

Video editing in Movie Maker

Windows Live Movie Maker is Microsoft's video-editing program for Windows 7, which can import, arrange, edit and share videos. You can download the Windows Live Movie Maker for free from http://download.live.com/moviemaker.

Help! Windows Live Movie Maker 2011 keeps crashing

If Movie Maker regularly freezes or crashes completely while working on a project there are a couple of things to try to fix the problems:

■ Divide your movie project into smaller bits. This helps the program better deal with resources and doesn't take up as much memory as it does trying to load a lengthy video.

■ Make sure your display drivers are fully up to date. To check this, click **Start**, and then click **Control Panel**. Click **System and Security**, and then click **Check for updates** in 'Windows Update'.

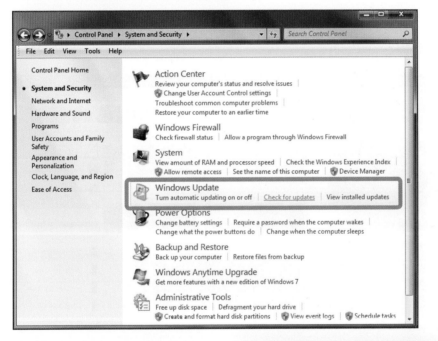

■ Try reinstalling Movie Maker. To do this, click **Start**, then click **Control Panel** and then click **Uninstall a program** in 'Programs'. From the list that appears, click **Windows Live Essentials** and then click **Uninstall** at the top of the column. Note this will also uninstall Windows Live Photo Gallery, although your photos will be untouched. Visit http://windows.microsoft.com/en-GB/windows-live/essentials-home to redownload Windows Live Movie Maker and Windows Live Photo Gallery.

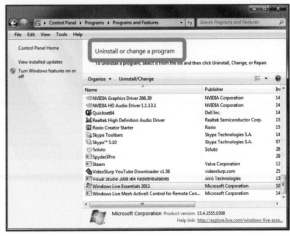

I can only view my movie in Windows Live Movie Maker

Check to see if the file extension of your movie is .wlmp. When you save a movie in Windows Live Movie Maker it is saved as a project file with the extension .wlmp. This means it can only be opened and viewed in Movie Maker. In order to share your video with friends and family via email, on CD or upload it to Facebook, YouTube or other websites, you must export it as a Windows Media Video or a .wmv file.

The easiest way to save your movie into a format that can be easily shared is to use one of the program's recommended settings. Windows Live Movie Maker will look at the size and bit rate of your source videos and then choose a setting that will produce the best balance between file size and video quality.

1 On the **Home** tab, in the 'Sharing' group, click **Save Movie**.

2 A drop-down menu appears that lists the recommended setting for the project together with common settings suitable for email, burning to DVD and so on.

3 Move your cursor over a setting to see more detail.

4 Choose a setting.

5 Pick a location to save the movie file and click **Save**.

BE CAREFUL!
Once you have published your video, you can't edit it. You can only edit the saved project, so make sure you're happy with it first.

I don't want to save my movie to Movie Maker's default settings. Can I use my own settings?

While Windows Live Movie Maker has many built-in settings, you can create a custom setting so you can save your movie at a quality level and size that meets your needs.

Create a custom setting

1 When you have finished editing your movie, on the **Home** tab, in the 'Sharing' group, click **Save Movie**.

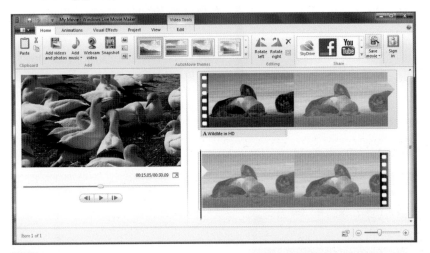

2 From the drop-down menu click **Create custom setting....**

Create Custom Setting

Setting: <New>

Name: My settings

Video settings

Width: 1280 pixels

Height: 720 pixels

Bit rate: 8000 kbps

Frame rate: 30 fps

Audio settings

Audio format: 128 kbps, 48 kHz, stereo

Estimated file size: 58.14 MB per minute of video

Delete | Save | Close

3 In the dialog box, type a name for the custom setting in the 'Name' box, such as 'My settings'.

4 Under 'Video settings', enter the video resolutions in the 'Width' and 'Height' fields. It's best to use the same size as of the source video size here.

5 Enter the bit rate you want to use for your video in 'Bit rate' box.

6 Enter the frame rate for your video in the 'Frame rate' box. This refers to the number of frames shown per second. The higher a frame rate a movie has the smoother it plays.

7 Select the 'Audio format' for your video.

8 Click **Save** and then **Save** again and then **Close** to quit the 'Create Custom Setting' dialog box.

Jargon buster

Bit rate Bit rate determines a movie's audio and video quality. The higher the bit rate, the better the quality but the file size of the movie will be bigger.

I can't add narration to play over a background audio track in my movie

By default, Microsoft Windows Movie Maker works with only one audio track at a time. You can add other audio files to a track and run them in sequence but not simultaneously. This can be frustrating when you want a piece of narration to play over a background audio file. However, there's a way to get around this restriction. Here's how to add a second audio track that plays simultaneously with the first track:

1 Finish your movie project with the first audio track. In this example, use the narration as the first track and set the music volume to **Maximum**.

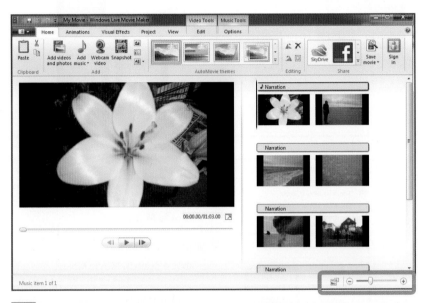

2 On the **Home** tab, click **Save movie**. This compiles the clips and audio track into a .wmv (movie) file.

3 Close Movie Maker.

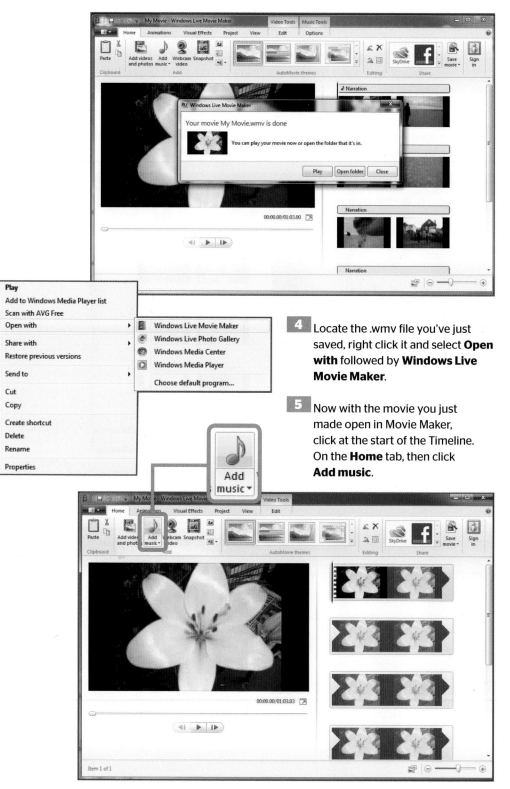

4 Locate the .wmv file you've just saved, right click it and select **Open with** followed by **Windows Live Movie Maker**.

5 Now with the movie you just made open in Movie Maker, click at the start of the Timeline. On the **Home** tab, then click **Add music**.

6 Select an audio track – in this example, 'Background song' – and click **Open**.

7 The second audio track will be added. You can preview it by playing the movie and adjust the volume as required. Then repeat Step 2 to save the movie once again.

I can't record video using my PC's built-in webcam

If you want to record a video of yourself using the webcam, it can be difficult using packages such as Skype. But if you're using Windows 7 and have downloaded Windows Live Essentials, you can record a video of yourself directly into Windows Live Movie Maker using its built-in webcam feature.

1 Click **Start**, then click **All Programs** and then double click **Windows Live Movie Maker**.

2 Click the **File** tab and select **Options**.

3 Click **Webcam** on the left-hand side of the dialog box and then select the audio device you want to use and the webcam device (in this example, the integrated webcam).

4 Click **OK**.

5 On the **Home** tab, click **Webcam video**.

6 Then click the red **Record** button to start recording your webcam live feed. When you have finished recording, click **Stop**.

7 Save your footage and it will be shown in the main movie window so you can edit the video as needed.

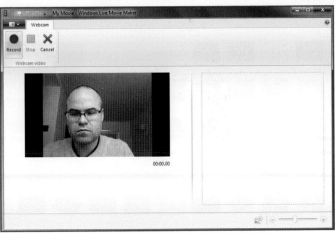

Help, I can't import video into Movie Maker

If you get an error message when trying to import video into Windows Live Movie Maker, the most likely reason is that it is in a format that isn't supported by the program or you don't have the correct codec installed on your computer. There are two solutions to this problem:

■ You can use a third-party – usually free – video converter to convert the existing video into a video format that will work with Windows Live Movie Maker.

■ Alternatively, if you know which codec you're missing, you can go to a codec manufacturer's website to download the most recent version. You can also download the most common codecs – many reputable sites offer free packs of the codecs – and install them yourself. Be careful to install the correct codecs for your version of Windows otherwise your video files may remain unrecognisable. If, for example, you're running a 64-bit version of Windows, you need to install 64-bit codecs.

> **Jargon buster**
> **Codec** A piece of software that's used to compress or decompress a digital media file, such as a song or video.

I can't add multiple effects to each slide

If you want to add more than one effect to your video, such as black and white effect and a blur effect, you can do this easily enough using Movie Makers' Multiple Effects feature.

1 Click **Start**, and then click **All programs** followed by **Windows Live Movie Maker**.

2 With the video loaded, click the desired clip and then click the **Visual Effects** tab.

3 Click the drop-down arrow to the far right of the effects icons. That will open up an expanded view of all the effects. Also along the bottom you should now see a button labelled 'Multiple Effects'.

4 Click the **Multiple Effects** button and then choose the multiple effects you'd like to apply.

If you frequently use multiple effects, you might want to right click on the icon next to 'Multiple Effects' and pin that to the Quick Access bar at the top.

Audio and video playing problems

Not being able to play your music or watch a video can be very frustrating – from audio that sounds terrible to not being able to find your music in Windows Media Player.

The audio from my PC sounds awful

Windows 7's sound controls are more than just a way to adjust the volume, they are handy to fix a range of audio problems. Beyond the speaker volume slider, you will find tools and settings that let you finely tune audio settings, helping you achieve the sound you are looking for. You can also adjust the sound levels for individual programs. So, for example, you can set the volume loud for Windows Media Player, while audio in Internet Explorer can play quietly. If you're experiencing sound issues – such as an individual program playing audio too loudly or quietly – then follow these steps:

One program is too loud, another is too quiet

1 Right click the **Speaker** icon on the notification area of the taskbar.

2 From the pop-up menu, click **Open Volume Mixer**.

3 Use the 'Speakers volume' slider to change the volume for your computer.

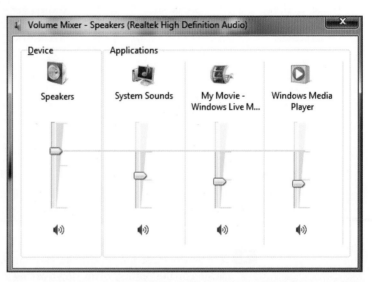

4 If you have any applications open and running, then you can use the Applications slider in the same 'Volume Mixer – Speakers' dialog box to adjust the volume for programs that use sounds. You can adjust each program separately, which can solve the headache of one program's volume being totally different to another application.

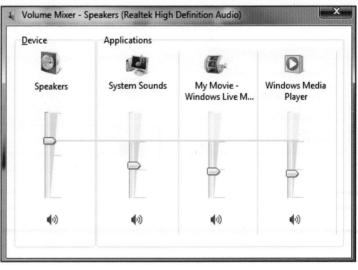

Fine-tune your speaker properties

1 In the 'Volume Mixer' dialog box, click the **Speakers** icon to launch the 'Speakers Properties' window.

2 Click the **Enhancements** tab to see the available enhancements. These include 'Environment', which simulates multiple playback environments, and 'Equalizer', which emulates the frequency response of different performances such as rock, pop and so forth.

3 For many of these enhancements, you can fine-tune their settings by then clicking on the 'Setting' **drop-down arrow** at the foot of the window. For example, Environment lets you choose the type of location where the sound will heard, helpful if you're in a spacious room or noisy environment.

Improve the audio quality

1 To get the best sound quality possible, open the 'Speakers Properties' window following Step 1 above, and then click the **Advanced** tab.

2 Here you can select your computer sound's sample rate and bit depth. Click the **drop-down arrow** to select a setting. The base setting is 16-bit CD Quality – try increasing it to 24-bit Studio Quality so your computer delivers better-quality audio.

I can't get audio when my computer is connected to my home cinema speakers

If you have external speakers connected to your PC, such as a home cinema 5.1 system, you can use Windows to take advantage of your surround sound set-up to get the best sound quality when watching films and playing games. However, Windows doesn't recognise this by default and you can be left with sound just coming from the computer's in-built speakers. To change this:

1 Right click the **Speaker** icon on the notification area of the taskbar.

2 From the pop-up menu click **Playback devices**.

Open Volume Mixer

Playback devices

Recording devices

Sounds

Volume control options

3 Click the **Speakers** icon and then click **Configure**.

4 In the 'Speaker Setup' window, select your speaker set-up from the list shown including Stereo (two speakers), 5.1 and 7.1 layouts, and click **Test**. You should hear a tone coming through each speaker.

5 Click **Next**, and then follow the steps in the wizard.

Configure Speakers

Test

Disable

Show Disabled Devices

✓ Show Disconnected Devices

About Software MIDI Synthesizer

Properties

Speaker Setup

Choose your configuration

Select the speaker setup below that is most like the configuration on your computer.

Audio channels:

Stereo

▶ Test

Click any speaker above to test it.

Next   Cancel

Tip

The options available during the speaker configuration process are determined by your PC's sound card and it's likely that you will see different options when configuring speakers on different computers. For movies and games, try to choose 5.1 as a setting if that matches your speaker set-up, for instance.

| Open Volume Mixer |
| Playback devices |
| Recording devices |
| **Sounds** |
| Volume control options |

Adjust Window sounds

You can adjust the sounds that your computer makes when Windows is doing different tasks.

1 Right click the **Speaker** icon on the notification area of the taskbar.

2 From the pop-up menu click **Sounds**.

3 To choose a sound scheme click the 'Windows Default' **drop-down arrow** and select a scheme from the menu.

4 To change a 'Program Event', click the event you'd like to change the sound for, then either select a Windows sound from the 'Sounds' drop-down menu or click **Browse...** to choose your own sound. To listen to a sound, click the **Test** button.

Sound dialog box:

Tabs: Playback | Recording | **Sounds** | Communications

A sound theme is a set of sounds applied to events in Windows and programs. You can select an existing scheme or save one you have modified.

Sound Scheme:

Windows Default | Save As... | Delete

To change sounds, click a program event in the following list and then select a sound to apply. You can save the changes as a new sound scheme.

Program Events:

- Windows
  - Asterisk
  - Close Program
  - Critical Battery Alarm
  - Critical Stop
  - Default Beep

☑ Play Windows Startup sound

Sounds:

(None) | ▶ Test | Browse...

OK | Cancel | Apply

Windows Media Player 12 doesn't update the library when I add an item to it

If items such as songs and audio aren't appearing or you encounter other issues with the Windows Media Player library, it may be that the media library database has become corrupted. You can refresh the library so it rebuilds itself. Just follow these steps:

1 Click **Start** and type **services.msc** in the search box. Click on **services** in the results list.

2 In the 'Services' dialog box that appears, find the service 'Windows Media Player Network Sharing Service' and select it.

Search results:

Programs (1)

services

See more results

services.msc ✕ | Shut down ►

Description:
Shares Windows Media Player libraries to other networked players and media devices using Universal Plug and Play

Services window:

Name	Description	Status	Startup Type	Log On As
Windows Firewall	Windows Fi...	Started	Automatic	Local Service
Windows Font Cache Service	Optimizes p...	Started	Automatic (Delaye...	Local Service
Windows Image Acquisition (WIA)	Provides im...	Started	Automatic	Local Service
Windows Installer	Adds, modi...		Manual	Local System
Windows Live Family Safety Service	This service ...	Started	Automatic	Local System
Windows Live ID Sign-in Assistant	Enables Win...	Started	Automatic	Local System
Windows Live Mesh remote connections service	Lets you co...		Disabled	Local System
Windows Management Instrumentation	Provides a c...	Started	Automatic	Local System
Windows Media Center Receiver Service	Windows M...		Manual	Network Service
Windows Media Center Scheduler Service	Starts and st...		Manual	Network Service
Windows Media Player Network Sharing Service	Shares Win...	Started	Automatic (Delaye...	Network Service
Windows Modules Installer	Enables inst...		Manual	Local System
Windows Presentation Foundation Font Cache 3....	Optimizes p...		Manual	Local Service
Windows Remote Management (WS-Management)	Windows R...		Manual	Network Service
Windows Search	Provides co...	Started	Automatic (Delaye...	Local System
Windows Time	Maintains d...		Manual	Local Service
Windows Update	Enables the ...	Started	Automatic (Delaye...	Local System
WinHTTP Web Proxy Auto-Discovery Service	WinHTTP i...	Started	Manual	Local Service
Wired AutoConfig	The Wired ...		Manual	Local System

\ Extended / Standard /

3 On the left side of the screen, click **Stop** to stop the service.

4 Keep the 'Services' window open as you will need it again later on to re-enable this service after you delete a few files. Open up Windows Explorer and navigate your way to: **C:\User\Username\AppData\Local\Microsoft\Media Player**.

5 From here delete all of the files named **CurrentDatabase_***.wmdb** and **LocalMLS_*.wmdb**. The '*' stands for a random number, the numbers will differ on each computer. There are only a few files, though, but make sure you delete them all.

6 Close the 'Explorer' window and click on the **Services** window. Right click the **Windows Media Player Network Sharing Service** and select **Start**. A small dialog box will temporarily appear while the process is being enabled.

7 Now all you have to do is open **Windows Media Player 12** and watch your library rebuild itself. Depending on the amount of songs you have and how fast your computer is, this process may take several minutes. Your missing songs should now appear in the list.

iTunes

iTunes is Apple's media player software that's used for playing, downloading, saving and organising digital music and video files on computers. It can also manage contents on iPods, iPhones, iPod Touches and iPads.

BE CAREFUL!

Make sure you back-up your iTunes library before you begin tinkering with any fixes. With iTunes open, click **File** then click **Library** and then click **Back up to Disc** and follow the instructions to back up to a blank DVD.

---

iTunes keeps crashing or freezing

If you use iTunes a lot – especially as a central library for your Apple iPod, iPhone or iPad to store your music, apps and video – then it can be frustrating if it keeps unexpectedly quitting, becomes unresponsive or simply won't open. If you're having no luck making iTunes work, try these easy fixes first.

Start iTunes in Safe Mode

iTunes has a Safe Mode that starts it in factory fresh condition, disabling extra plug-ins and scripts that may have been added that are causing problems. To start in Safe Mode:

1 Click **Start**, then click **All Programs** and locate Apple iTunes.

2 Hold down the **Shift** and **Control** keys, then double click **iTunes** to launch it. If you're successful, you will see the message 'iTunes is running in safe mode'. Click Continue.

iTunes is running in safe mode.
Visual plug-ins you have installed have been temporarily disabled.

Continue   Quit

3 Check if iTunes is working as needed – if it is, then it might be a plug-in that is the cause of the problem. To remove plug-ins, go to the iTunes plug-in folder, which is located at **C:\Program Files\iTunes\iTunes Plug-ins and at C:\Users\username\App Data\Roaming\Apple Computer\iTunes\ iTunes Plug-ins**. Try moving plug-ins temporarily and one by one to the desktop and then restart iTunes each time to identify the plug-in that is causing problems.

Create a new user account

If you're still experiencing issues, then it's worth creating a new user account in Windows 7 and running iTunes from the new user account. This will determine if the problem is connected to the user account or if it is a system-wide problem.

1 Click **Start**, then click **Control Panel**.

2 Click **Open or remove user accounts**, then click **Create a new account** and follow the instructions to create the account. Once the account is created, choose **Log Off** from the **Start** menu, then log into the new user account.

3 Launch iTunes, and see if the problem has been resolved. If it has, then the problem is a user-specific iTunes problem and you should follow the steps in the section below and overleaf to page 185 relating to this.

Try some fixes
If you followed the steps in 'Create a new user account' and iTunes works fine in the new account, then log back into your original user account and try the following fixes:

▪ **Remove the iTunes preferences file**. Some iTunes files that store preferences and settings may be corrupted. There are two folders that store these files, and by moving them from their original location to the desktop may fix the issue.

1 Click the **Windows Explorer** icon on the taskbar and navigate to **C:\users\ username\AppData\Local\Apple Computer\iTunes** and move the 'Preferences' folder to the desktop. Relaunch iTunes and see if that solves the problem.

2 If not, then replace the folder you have just moved back to its original location and move to the next section.

Create a new iTunes library

1 Click **Start**, then locate iTunes and press and hold the **Shift** key before launching iTunes.

2 In the 'Choose iTunes Library' prompt, choose **Create Library...** and select a location to save the new iTunes library. Then click **Save**.

iTunes		x
♫ **Choose iTunes Library**		
iTunes needs a library to continue. You may choose an existing iTunes library or create a new one.		
Quit	Choose Library...	Create Library...

3 Check if iTunes works with the new library. If it does, then relaunch iTunes while holding the **Shift** key and select your original library.

Re-create your iTunes library.
The problem may be caused by an unstable iTunes library, and one option is to rebuild it. It's worth noting that any devices that you connect with iTunes, such as an iPod, will completely resync after you have rebuilt the library.

1 If iTunes is open, then quit it. Click the **Windows Explorer** icon on the taskbar and navigate to the iTunes folder at **C:\users\username\My Music\iTunes**.

2 Locate the file **Library.itl** and move it to the desktop.

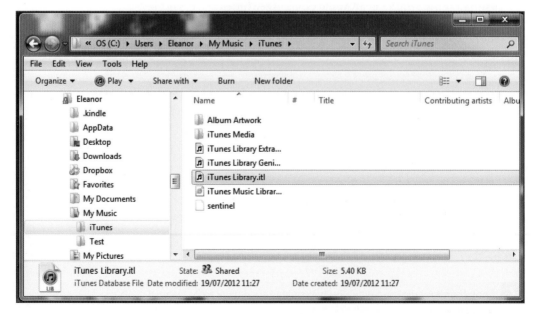

3 Open iTunes, and you should not see any content listed. Click **File** and click **Add Folder to Library...**, then navigate to the folder that holds your music. It is typically located at **C:\users\username\My Music\iTunes\iTunes Media**.

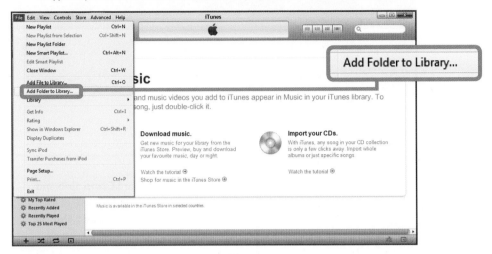

4 Individually add an artist, song or album to the library, and continue adding content one at a time. If you encounter a problem when adding a specific song or album, then you have located the problem file that is causing iTunes issues. Repeat Steps 1-4, but do not add the problem file this time around. iTunes should now work fine, and you'll need to delete the problem file.

I've updated or just installed iTunes, and now it refuses to work

Sometimes iTunes won't work after you have updated it, or if you perform a fresh install. Perform these steps to see if it fixes the problem:

1 Click **Start**, then click **Computer**. In the 'Organize' menu, click **Folder and Search Options** and then click the **View** tab.

2 In the 'Advanced settings' pane at the lower-half of the window, click **Hidden files and folders** and then ensure that 'Show hidden files, folders, and drives' is selected and click **OK**.

3 Click the **Windows Explorer** icon on the taskbar and navigate to **C:\ProgramData\Apple Computer\iTunes\SC Info**.

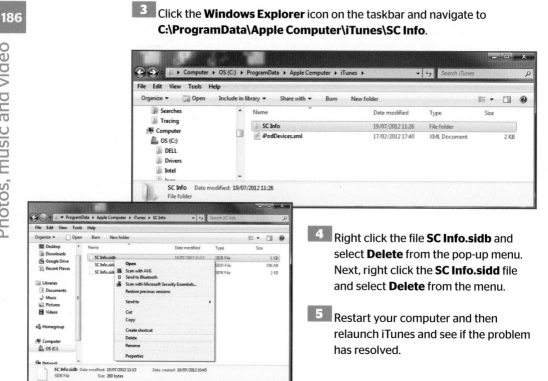

4 Right click the file **SC Info.sidb** and select **Delete** from the pop-up menu. Next, right click the **SC Info.sidd** file and select **Delete** from the menu.

5 Restart your computer and then relaunch iTunes and see if the problem has resolved.

I have update to the latest version of iTunes but now my music is missing

If after downloading and installing the latest version of iTunes, your music, video and other content fail to show, try these steps:

1 Quit iTunes. In **Windows Explorer** navigate to find the iTunes folder that contains the library files **C:\Users\username\ My Music\iTunes**.

2 Drag the **iTunes Library** file from the above location to the desktop. Open the **Previous iTunes Libraries** folder in the 'iTunes' folder.

3 Locate the file named **iTunes Library YYYY-MM-DD** where YYYY-MM-DD is the date you upgraded iTunes (Year-Month-Day).

4 Drag this file to the **iTunes** folder where you removed the iTunes Library file from in Step 3. Rename this file to **iTunes Library**.

5 Open iTunes. You should now see your missing content in iTunes.

Syncing problems

By reading this chapter you'll get to grips with:

- Syncing with iPods, iPhones and iPads
- Syncing with android devices

Syncing with iPods, iPhones and iPads

Computers are increasingly playing host to a vast amount of digital content, including music, apps and videos that you can then move onto devices such as Apple iPods for listening to music on the move, for example. But if your iPod won't connect to iTunes or your computer, it can affect the use of your iPod. Here are some of the more common syncing problems you will encounter.

My iPhone or iPod Touch is not appearing in iTunes

If you have connected your iPod or iPhone via USB to your computer and launched iTunes, your device will appear on the left-hand column of iTunes. If it doesn't appear, then try these steps to fix the issue:

Update iTunes

Making sure you have the latest version of iTunes is a good idea, as often Apple will release new versions that fix potential problems including syncing issues with your iPod or iPhone.

1 Click **Start**, and click **All Programs** to locate iTunes. Double click it to launch.

2 Click on the **Help** menu, and then click **Check for Updates**. If there's a new version of iTunes available, click OK to download and install it.

Restart your iPod or iPhone

The syncing problem may be to do with a conflict on your iPod or iPhone, which can be fixed by restarting the device. To restart the iPod or iPhone, press and hold the **Sleep/Wake** button on the top-edge of the device until a red slider appears on the screen. Slide your finger across the slider to turn off the device. Next, press and hold the **Sleep/Wake** button until the Apple logo appears and try reconnecting again.

If it still isn't syncing, you can reset the iPod or iPhone by pressing and holding the **Sleep/Wake** button and the **Home** button on the front of the device. Keep pressing and holding both buttons until the device shuts down and a silver

Apple logo appears on the screen. Release both buttons when it appears and, when the iPod or iPhone has finished restarting, try to connect it to your computer.

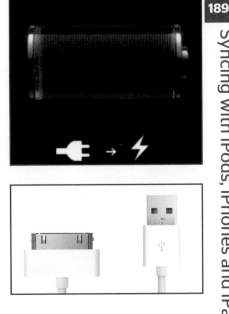

Check the power level

One reason why an iPod or iPhone won't sync with your computer is that the battery power may be very low. If it's very low, the display will appear blank for up to five minutes, and it may not show up on iTunes. Connect your iPhone or iPod to the power charger and charge for at least 20 minutes before trying to connect it to iTunes.

Check the USB connections

If your iPod Touch or iPhone is still not appearing in iTunes, check the USB connections by unplugging everything and reconnecting. If you can, connect the device to a USB port built into the computer rather than through a USB hub or USB port on a keyboard. Try a different USB port if iTunes is still not seeing your device.

Restart your computer

You can try restarting your Windows 7 computer before reconnecting your iPod Touch or iPhone using a USB cable.

Reinstall iTunes

If all else fails, it is worth completely removing iTunes from Windows 7 and reinstalling from scratch. Don't worry – you shouldn't lose any of your music, videos or apps, but to be on the safe side, create a backup of your iTunes library (see Be Careful! on page 182). It's worth noting that these steps for reinstalling iTunes will take some time to complete.

1 Click **Start**, then click **Control Panel** and in the 'Programs' box click **Uninstall a program**.

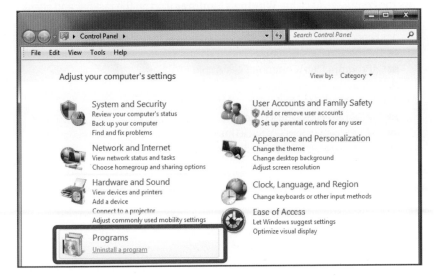

2 In the window that appears, locate the program **iTunes** and click **Uninstall** from the top menu. Repeat the process, uninstalling the following list of programs in the exact order:

■ QuickTime
■ Apple Software Update
■ Apple Mobile Devices Support
■ Bonjour
■ Apple Application Support

← → ▽ ▣ ▸ Control Panel ▸ Programs ▸ Programs and Features	▼	↵	Search Programs and Features	🔎

File   Edit   View   Tools   Help

Control Panel Home

View installed updates

Turn Windows features on or off

Uninstall or change a program

To uninstall a program, select it from the list and then click Uninstall, Change, or Repair.

Organize ▾   **Uninstall**   Change   Repair   ▦ ▾   ❓

Uninstall this program.

Name	Publisher	In:
📖 Intel® HD Graphics Driver	Intel Corporation	15
📖 Intel® Management Engine Components	Intel Corporation	15
🎵 iTunes	Apple Inc.	09
🔷 Java(TM) 6 Update 24 (64-bit)	Oracle	14
🔷 Java(TM) 6 Update 33	Oracle	24
🔲 Juniper Networks Host Checker	Juniper Networks	19
🔲 Juniper Networks Secure Application Manager	Juniper Networks	02
🔲 Juniper Networks Setup Client	Juniper Networks	19
🔲 Juniper Networks Setup Client Activex Control	Juniper Networks	19

Apple Inc.   Product version: 10.6.3.25

Help link: http://www.apple.com/uk/support/

3 You need to confirm that the programs were successfully removed from the computer. Click the **Windows Explorer** icon on the taskbar and check that the following folders and their contents are no longer on your PC. If you encounter any of the folders listed below, then delete them:

■ C:\Program Files\Bonjour
■ C:\Program Files\Common Files\Apple
■ C:\Program Files\iTunes
■ C:\Program Files\iPod
■ C:\Program Files\QuickTime
■ C:\Windows\System32\QuickTime
■ C:\Windows\System32\QuickTimeVR

If you're running a 64-bit version of Windows, you will also need to check the following folders were deleted:

- C:\Program Files (x86)\Bonjour
- C:\Program Files (x86)\Common Files\Apple
- C:\Program Files (x86)\iTunes
- C:\Program Files (x86)\iPod
- C:\Program Files (x86)\QuickTime
- C:\Windows\SysWOW64\QuickTime
- C:\Windows\SysWOW64\QuickTimeVR

Tip

To check what version of Windows you're using, click **Start**, then right click **Computer** and click **Properties**. The lower part of the window will display the version (32-bit or 64-bit) that your version of Windows is.

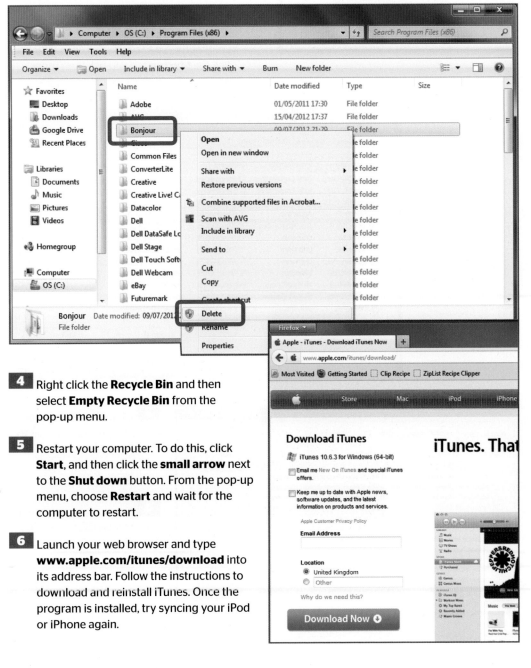

4 Right click the **Recycle Bin** and then select **Empty Recycle Bin** from the pop-up menu.

5 Restart your computer. To do this, click **Start**, and then click the **small arrow** next to the **Shut down** button. From the pop-up menu, choose **Restart** and wait for the computer to restart.

6 Launch your web browser and type **www.apple.com/itunes/download** into its address bar. Follow the instructions to download and reinstall iTunes. Once the program is installed, try syncing your iPod or iPhone again.

Check for software conflicts

Some anti-virus and security software can prevent your iPod or iPhone from being detected by iTunes. You can use 'msconfig' to see if there are software issues preventing you from successfully syncing your iPod or iPhone.

1 To show what programs run at startup, click **Start** and type **msconfig** in the search box. In the results panel above the box, click the program **msconfig**.

2 The 'System Configuration' window will appear. Click the **General** tab and make sure that the 'Load startup items' is unticked. Click the **Startup** tab and tick the 'iTunes' and 'QuickTime' check boxes on the list.

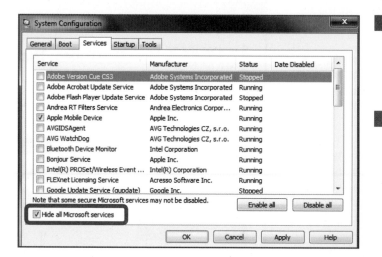

3 Click the **Services** tab, and place a tick next to 'Hide All Microsoft Services', then click **Disable all**.

4 Place a tick in the 'Apple Mobile Device' check box, then click **OK**.

5 Restart your computer (see page 191).

6 When your computer restarts, you may see an error message 'Windows has blocked some startup programs'. Click the message, then click the **Blocked startup programs** icon. If you don't see the message, move to Step 9.

7 Select **Run blocked program** from the pop-up menu that appears, and then select **System Configuration Utility**.

8 Click **OK** in the window that appears with the message 'You have used the System Configuration Utility to make changes to the way Windows starts'. The 'System Configuration' utility will appear – do not click OK.

9 Try to sync your iPod or iPhone with iTunes. If it works, then you need to use 'System Configuration' utility to turn on third-party 'System Services and Startup' items one at a time to understand which startup or system services is causing a syncing conflict, restarting your computer each time and seeing if you can still connect your device to iTunes. Once identified, you should ensure that the conflicting startup item is disabled in the 'System Configuration' utility so you can successfully sync with iTunes.

I can't sync apps I purchased on my iPhone to my computer

If you have bought apps from the iTunes App Store on your iPhone (or iPod Touch or iPad), and are having trouble syncing them to your computer try the following steps:

1 Click **Start** and click **All Programs** to locate iTunes, then launch it. Connect your iPhone, iPod Touch or iPad and wait for the sync to finish. If the apps you purchased on your iPhone did not transfer to your PC, then right click on the iPhone or iPod in the left-hand pane and select **Transfer purchases** from the pop-up menu.

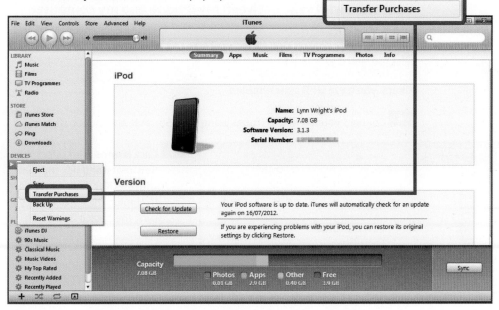

2 If that doesn't work, then click **iTunes Store** in the left-hand pane, and go to the **App Store** and click on the **Purchased** link on the right-hand side of the window.

3 On the **Purchased** screen, click the **Apps** icon. This will show a list of all the apps you have purchased on your iPod, iPhone or iPad or on your Windows computer.

4 Select the app you want to download, and click the small **Cloud with down arrow** icon to download it to you computer.

5 Click **File** and then click **Transfer purchases from...** to sync all your purchases.

I can't use wi-fi sync between my iPhone and my computer

A new feature of iOS 5 running on iPhones, iPod Touch and iPads is wi-fi sync, which attempts to sync your device wirelessly to your Windows 7 computer. If it isn't working properly, try these fixes:

Check you have wi-fi sync enabled

1 Connect your device to iTunes using the USB cable and launch iTunes.

2 Click **iTunes** then select **Summary** and tick the 'Sync with this iOS device over wi-fi'. Unplug the cable and try to sync the device using wi-fi.

Check Windows Firewall isn't holding things up

Windows Firewall may be the culprit behind the lack of syncing over wi-fi, but a quick fix can solve that:

1 Click the **Start** button, and then click **Control Panel**.

2 Click **System and security** and then click **Allow a program through Windows Firewall**.

3 In the list that appears, look for 'SyncServer' and make sure there is a tick next to it.

4 If it's missing, click **Change Settings** and then click **Allow another program…**. Click **Browse**.

5 In the file box that appears, navigate to **C:\Program Files\ Common Files\Apple\ Mobile Device Support\SyncServer. exe** and click **OK**.

6 Restart iTunes and your device should appear using a wi-fi connection.

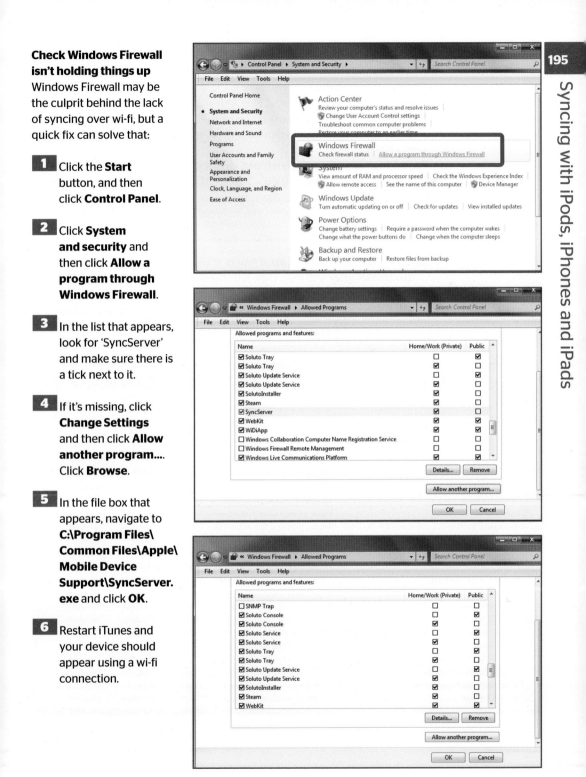

Syncing with Android devices

Unlike iPhones and iPads, Google-powered Android tablets and smartphones are designed to be entirely self-sufficient and don't need to sync to a computer. However, it's possible to sync your files with your PC, which can solve many problems when it comes to managing your media. The best route is to sync with Windows Media Player in Windows 7, but you can run into problems.

When I try to sync my Android device, Windows Media Player says it synced successfully – but nothing actually was synced!
If you're using Windows Media Player connected to the 'My Music' folder to sync music from your Windows 7 PC and an Android device, this can be a common problem. To overcome this:

1 Click **Start**, then click **Control Panel**. In the Search box, type **troubleshooter** and then click **Troubleshooting** from the results list.

2 Click **View all**, and then click **Windows Media Player Library** and follow the instructions to check if Windows Media Player is correctly installed or if the Player Library is broken. Follow the steps to fix any problems.

			Troubleshooting ▸ All Categories	▾	✦	Search Troubleshooting		🔎

File   Edit   View   Tools   Help

Troubleshoot computer problems

Name	Description	Location	Category	Publisher	
Internet Connections	Connect to the Internet or to a pa...	Local	Network	Microsoft ...	
Network Adapter	Troubleshoot Ethernet, wireless, ...	Local	Network	Microsoft ...	
Performance	Adjust settings to help improve o...	Online	Performan...	Microsoft ...	
Playing and Burning CDs, DVDs, and Blu-ray Discs	Resolve problems that prevent pl...	Online	Device	Microsoft ...	
Playing Audio	Play sounds and other audio suc...	Local	Sound	Microsoft ...	
Power	Adjust power settings to help im...	Local	Power	Microsoft ...	
Printer	Troubleshoot problems preventin...	Local	Printing	Microsoft ...	
Program Compatibility	Make older programs run in this ...	Local	Programs	Microsoft ...	
Recording Audio	Record audio input from a micro...	Local	Sound	Microsoft ...	
Search and Indexing	Find items on your computer usi...	Local	Windows	Microsoft ...	▤
Set up TV tuner	Troubleshoot problems that prev...	Online	Windows	Microsoft ...	
Shared Folders	Access shared files and folders on...	Local	Network	Microsoft ...	
System Maintenance	Clean up unused files and shortc...	Local	System	Microsoft ...	
Windows Media Player DVD	Play a DVD using Windows Media...	Local	Media Pla...	Microsoft ...	
Windows Media Player Library	Make media files show up in the ...	Local	Media Pla...	Microsoft ...	
Windows Media Player Settings	Reset Windows Media Player to d...	Local	Media Pla...	Microsoft ...	
Windows Update	Resolve problems that prevent yo...	Online	Windows	Microsoft ...	▾

Essential advice

By reading this chapter you'll get to grips with:

- Keeping files safely backed up and restoring your PC if things go wrong
- Updating and reinstalling Windows 7
- Setting up a firewall to protect your computer

Backup your files

Windows 7 has a 'Backup and Restore' feature that you can use to create digital copies of your files and folders, keeping them safe if your computer crashes or you accidently delete files. You will need to have an external hard drive attached to the computer to back up your files before starting.

Use Windows 7 automatic backup

1 Click **Start**, then click **Control Panel**. In the 'Control Panel' window, click **System and Security**, then click **Backup and Restore**.

2 Click **Set up backup**, then follow the steps in the on-screen back-up wizard. You may need to enter your administrator password at this point.

You can search for backed-up files in the 'Backup and Restore' panel. Click **Search**, then type all or part of a file name, then click **Search**.

Jargon buster
External hard drive A storage device that plugs into your PC. Useful for saving copies of important files or creating additional storage.

Windows will then create a backup according to the settings you made during the set-up. It's worth noting that backing up your data can take a while, so leave it to run until it has completed the backup.

You should schedule regular backups when setting up the 'Backup and Restore' wizard so your work is regularly protected. Windows will then backup any new data you have added or changes to files onto the external storage at regular intervals that you determine.

Create an instant backup
Even if you have created a back-up schedule, you can override it and perform an instant backup when you want to.

1 Click **Start**, then click **Control Panel**. In the 'Control Panel' window, click **System and Security**, then click **Backup and Restore**.

2 Click **Back up now**. You may need to enter your administrator password at this point.

Restore backed-up files
If your files have been deleted, changed accidently or you need to restore the files you have previously backedup, follow these steps:

1 Click **Start**, then click **Control Panel**. In the 'Control Panel' window, click **System and Security**, then click **Backup and Restore**.

2 Click **Restore my files**.

3 If you want to restore just a few specific files, click **Browse for files** or **Browse for folders**. Choose the ones to backup.

Make a System Repair Disc

If something goes badly wrong with your computer, it is important to have created a System Repair Disc – and this is especially useful if you can't start your computer from its internal hard drive. This can help you fix Windows 7 if a major error occurs, and is used if you don't have access to a Windows 7 installation disc or the recovery options – such as a recovery CD – that was supplied with your computer.

Create a System Repair Disc

A System Repair Disc can be created at any time – all you need to be able to do this is a blank CD or DVD.

1 Click **Start**, then click **Control Panel**.

2 Click **System and Security**, then click **Backup and Restore**.

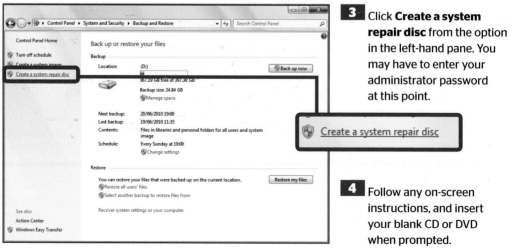

3 Click **Create a system repair disc** from the option in the left-hand pane. You may have to enter your administrator password at this point.

4 Follow any on-screen instructions, and insert your blank CD or DVD when prompted.

Use the System Repair Disc

If you're faced with a major computer problem such as the computer not starting from its internal hard drive, you can use the System Repair Disc to restore Windows.

1 Place the system repair disc into your CD or DVD drive.

2 Restart by pressing the computer's power button.

3 If prompted, press any key to start the computer from the System Repair Disc.

4 Confirm or change any Language settings, then click **Next**.

5 Select the **Startup Repair** option, and then click **Next**.

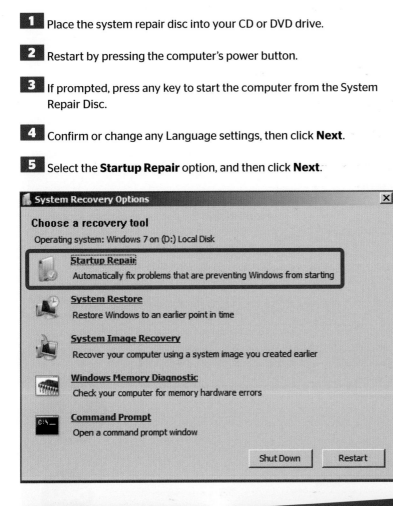

To submit a question to the Which? Computing Helpdesk, go to **www.which.co.uk/computinghelpdesk** and enter the following code where it asks for a membership number: **COMPSOLVE12**.

If Windows asks you to install a Windows installation disc, it means that your computer doesn't have the necessary files on its hard drive to create a System Repair Disc. You will need to insert your Windows 7 installation disc to continue.

Restore your computer

If you experience a major system crash or software problem, you can use Windows 7 System Restore to return the PC's system files and programs to a time when everything was working properly.

System Restore uses 'restore points' that act like markers for your PC. They can be created to a schedule and you should make a restore point before a major task such as installing software. If you need to, you can then use System Restore to return your PC to how it was when it saved a 'restore point'.

Set up System Restore

Before you use System Restore, save all open files and close all running applications. Once a restore point is set, your computer will automatically restart itself, so only start this process when you're ready.

1 Click **Start**, then right click **Computer**. Click **Properties** in the pop-up menu that appears.

2 Click **System protection** in the left-hand pane. You may have to enter your administrator password at this point.

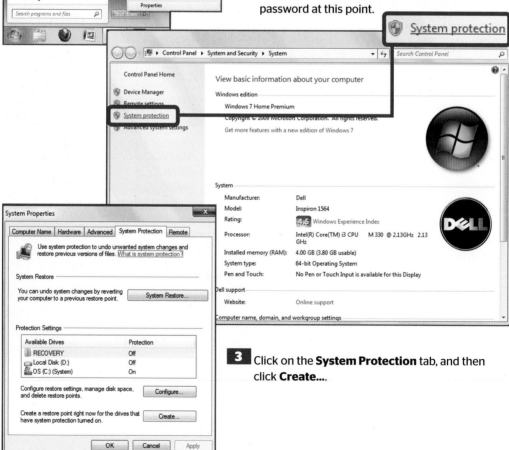

3 Click on the **System Protection** tab, and then click **Create....**

4 Enter a description such as 'Restore point September 29, 2012' in the 'System Protection' dialog box, then click **Create**.

> System Protection
>
> Create a restore point
>
> Type a description to help you identify the restore point. The current date and time are added automatically.
>
> Restore point September 29, 2012
>
> Create   Cancel

A restore point will now be automatically created and your computer will then restart. Once restarted, you can use your computer as normal and, if you encounter a problem, you can return your computer to the state it was in when you created the restore point.

Choose a restore point to return your computer to

If your computer starts experiencing problems – such as after you have installed new software – you can use a system restore point. System Restore will recommend the most recently created restore point, but you can choose a different one based on a time and date, such as before you installed the problematic software. It's a good idea to use of the restore point description as detailed in Step 4 above, so you can label the restore with information before you do something significant to your PC.

Use System Restore to recover your computer

If you do need to return the state of your computer to that of a previous restore point, follow these steps:

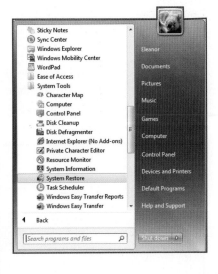

1 Click **Start**, then choose **All programs**. Navigate to **Accessories**, then **System Tools** in the menu.

2 Click on **System Restore**, then click **Next** in the Restore system files and settings window.

> System Restore
>
> Restore system files and settings
>
> System Restore can help fix problems that might be making your computer run slowly or stop responding.
>
> System Restore does not affect any of your documents, pictures, or other personal data. Recently installed programs and drivers might be uninstalled. Is this process reversible?
>
> < Back   Next >   Cancel

3 From the menu that appears, choose the restore point you'd like to return your computer to, such as the state it was in when you created the restore point: 'Restore point September 29, 2012'.

4 Click **Next**, then click **Finish** on the 'Confirm your restore point' window to begin restoring your computer.

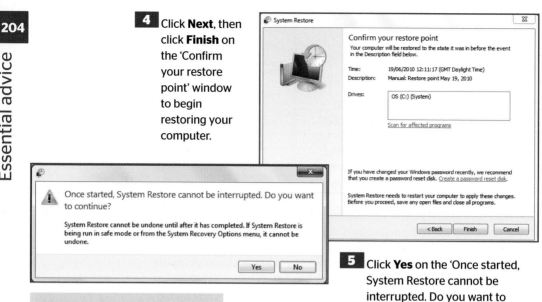

5 Click **Yes** on the 'Once started, System Restore cannot be interrupted. Do you want to continue?' message.

Tip
System Restore only affects Windows 7 files such as system files, programs and other settings. It does not affect your personal data such as email, photos and documents.

It may take several minutes, but Windows 7 will be restored to the state it was in at the restore point you selected in Step 3. Once done, your computer will then shut down and restart.

Can I reverse the changes System Restore makes?

If you use a restore point by mistake, it's not a problem. System Restore creates a second restore point automatically so you can rewind your computer back to the place before you used a restore point by mistake. To undo a restore point:

1 Click **Start**, then choose **All programs**. Navigate to **Accessories**, then **System Tools** in the menu.

2 Click on **System Restore**. You may have to enter your administrator password at this point.

3 Click **Undo System Restore**, and then click **Next**. If you're happy with your decision, click **Finish** and the restore point you accidently created will be erased.

Storing System restore points

System restore points are saved until the space allocated on your hard drive for keeping restore points is used up. If it runs out of space, the newest restore points will automatically overwrite the oldest restore points.

If you can't see your restore point, tick the 'Show more restore points' box to see more than just the most recent restore points.

Update Windows and programs

Keeping your computer up-to-date will help fix glitches and niggles, as well as ensure that you're protected from faults and problems as they're discovered. Windows 7 has an automatic updating facility that ensures updates are downloaded and installed as they become available.

To keep your PC healthy, it's a good idea to set Windows Update to automatically check and download new driver updates, and to install them without you needing to do anything. Windows Update will only download and install important or recommended updates – you will have to install optional updates manually following the steps below.

1 Ensure that you're connected to the internet.

2 Click **Start** and type **update** in the search box. Click on **Windows Update** in the list of results.

3 Click **Change settings** in the left pane.

4 Click on an item in the list under Important updates to determine which updates to automatically download and install.

5 Tick the 'Give me recommended updates the same way I receive important updates' in the 'Recommended updates' section, then click **OK**. You may have to enter your administrator password at this point.

Programs (3)
- Apple Software Update
- Check For Update
- Windows Update

Control Panel (18)
- Update device drivers
- Check for updates
- Turn automatic updating on or off
- View installed updates
- Device Manager
- View recent messages about your computer

Files (9)
- p186 - Using Windows Update to install drivers - step 6
- p186 - Using Windows Update to install drivers - step 4
- p186 - Using Windows Update to install drivers - step 3
- p186 - Using Windows Update to install drivers - step 1-2
- p184 - I'm having problems installing updates automatically - s...
- p184 - I'm having problems installing updates automatically - s...

See more results

upda   ×   Shut down ►

« Windows Update ► Change settings   ▼ | ↔ | Search Control Panel

Choose how Windows can install updates

When your computer is online, Windows can automatically check for important updates and install them using these settings. When new updates are available, you can also install them before shutting down the computer.

How does automatic updating help me?

Important updates

Install updates automatically (recommended)

Install new updates: Every day   ▼   at 03:00 ▼

Recommended updates
☑ Give me recommended updates the same way I receive important updates

Who can install updates
☑ Allow all users to install updates on this computer

Microsoft Update
☑ Give me updates for Microsoft products and check for new optional Microsoft software when I update Windows

Software notifications
☐ Show me detailed notifications when new Microsoft software is available

Note: Windows Update might update itself automatically first when checking for other updates. Read our privacy statement online.

Recommended updates
☑ Give me recommended updates the same way I receive important updates

OK   Cancel

I'm having problems installing updates automatically

If you have set up automatic Windows updates, but you're having problems downloading them or installing them, use the Windows 'Update troubleshooter' to fix common problems that can occur with Windows Update.

1 Click **Start**, then click **Control Panel**.

2 Type **troubleshooter** in the 'Control Panel' search box, and click **Troubleshooting** in the list of results that appear.

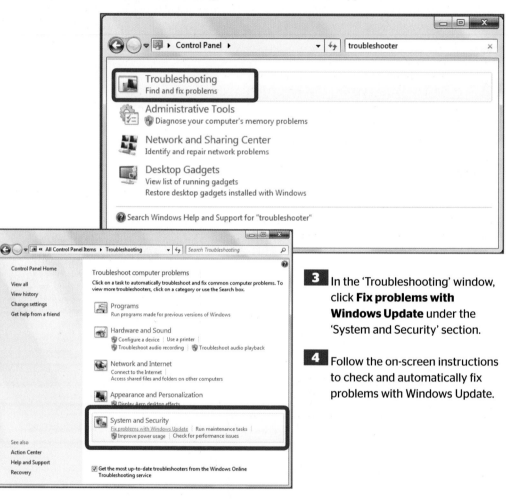

3 In the 'Troubleshooting' window, click **Fix problems with Windows Update** under the 'System and Security' section.

4 Follow the on-screen instructions to check and automatically fix problems with Windows Update.

Windows Update keeps restarting my computer

This is normal once an update has been downloaded and installed. Once finished, Windows will show a message saying that it needs to restart Windows to finish the update process.

If you don't want Windows to restart your computer straight away, click the **Postpone the restart** option. It's worth knowing that if you leave your computer unattended for a long period while Windows Update downloads and updates Windows, it will automatically restart the computer after a set time.

Update drivers

In many cases, issues with your computer not working properly can be traced back to problems with drivers. A driver is a small program that tells Windows and other software how to talk to a piece of hardware, such as how to print out a web page to your printer.

If a hardware device isn't working properly, you may need to update the driver. It's good practice to routinely look to update your drivers to help keep your PC healthy.

> You can let anyone who uses your computer install updates by ticking the 'Allow all users to install updates on this computer' in Windows Update.

Options for updating drivers

- Windows Update can be set to automatically download and install recommended updates, including the latest drivers for your devices.
- You can often install a driver from any DVD or CD from the manufacturer that came with the hardware, such as a printer. This is handy for restoring the driver back to its 'factory settings'.
- You can download and update the driver yourself from the manufacturer's websites. This is useful if Windows Update can't locate the driver for your device, and you can't locate a DVD or CD that includes the driver.

Using Windows Update to install drivers

Windows Update can be checked at any time to see if a new, updated driver has been made available for your particular device.

1 Ensure that you're connected to the internet.

2 Click **Start** and type **update** in the search box. Click on **Windows Update** in the list of results.

3 Click **Check for updates** in the left-hand pane. Windows Update will check online to see if there are any updates available. Click the links to see

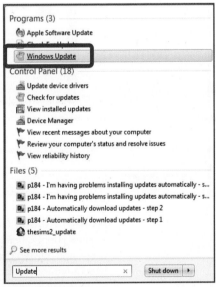

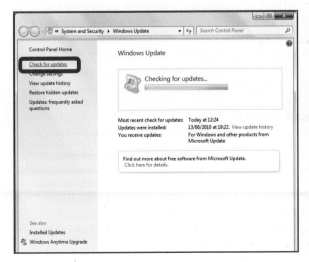

more information about any available updates. You can also see if an update is listed as important, recommended or optional for your device. Drivers will be included in all types of available update.

4 Click on the **Select the updates you want** to install page, and identify the updates relevant to your hardware devices.

5 Tick the box next to each driver that you want to install and update, and then click **OK**.

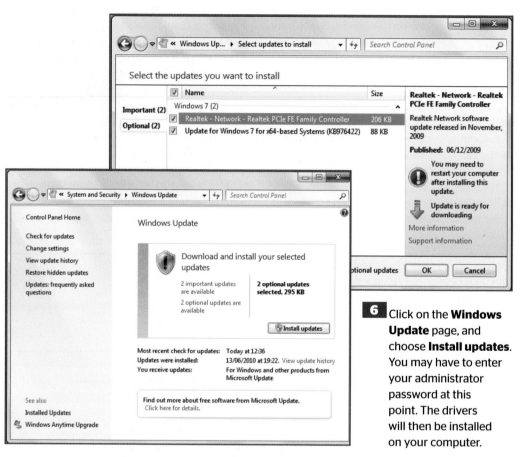

6 Click on the **Windows Update** page, and choose **Install updates**. You may have to enter your administrator password at this point. The drivers will then be installed on your computer.

Automatically install recommended updates to drivers

To keep your PC healthy, it's a good idea to set Windows Update to automatically check and download new driver updates, and to install them without you needing to do anything. Windows Update will only download and install important or recommended updates only – you will have to install optional updates manually following the steps below and opposite.

Manually download drivers

While it's a good idea to let Windows Update take care of updating software and drivers automatically, sometimes you have to find a driver manually online.

1 Make sure you're connected to the internet, and use your web browser to go to the website of the manufacturer of your hardware device.

2 Search in the support section of the website to locate and download the driver you need.

3 Once located and downloaded, follow the installation instructions on the website. Most drivers will install themselves automatically when they are downloaded – you just need to double click on the downloaded driver to start the installation process.

Manually install drivers

If the driver doesn't automatically install in Step 3 (above), then you can install it manually. You will need to be logged in as an administrator to do this.

Tip
If you're buying a new device, such as a printer, go to the Windows 7 Compatibility Center online. It holds a list of devices that have been tested to work with Windows 7.

1 Click **Start**, then click **Control Panel**.

2 In the 'Control Panel' window, click **System and Security**, then in the 'System' section, click **Device Manager**. You may have to enter your administrator password at this point.

3 Find the device you want to update the driver for in the list of hardware categories, and double click the device name.

4 Click the **Driver** tab, then click **Update Driver...**. Follow the installation instructions to locate the driver and install it.

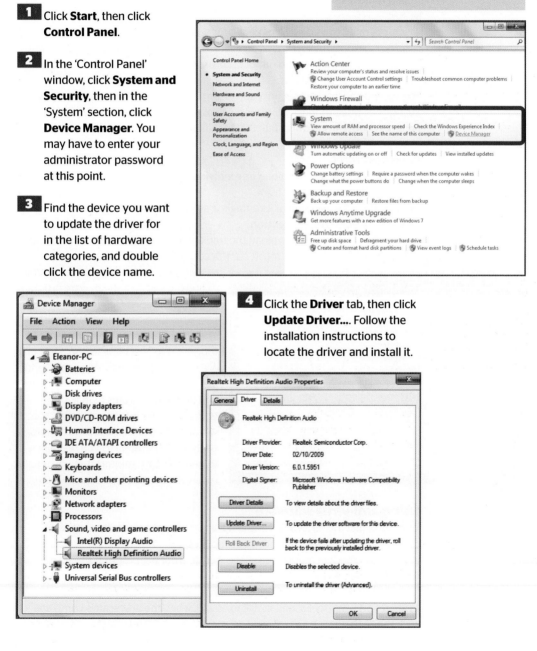

Install security software

The best way to protect your computer against external threats such as viruses and spyware is to have three types of security software installed on your computer. You need to have:

■ **A firewall.** This acts as a guard to protect your computer from incoming attacks from the internet.

■ **Anti-virus software.** A virus is a program that can infect your computer resulting in it slowing down, losing data or becoming corrupted. Anti-virus software helps to protect against viruses, trojans and worms by scanning for and removing infected files.

■ **Anti-spyware software.** Spyware is malicious software that downloads to your computer without your knowledge. It can monitor your activity, collect information about you and even hijack your browser. Anti-spyware software scans your computer and removes any spyware it finds.

You can buy an internet security suite from a high street computer store, which includes all three of these programs. As new viruses are identified every day, it helps to choose a software suite that includes an automatic update capability.

Free software

Alternatively, you can download free individual programs from the internet and there are several to choose from.

■ AVG offer a free version of its anti-virus software. Go to www.free.avg.com and click **Get basic protection**.

■ Windows 7 users can download the free anti-virus program Microsoft Security Essentials from www.microsoft.com/Security_Essentials.

■ Windows 7 also comes with a built-in firewall and an anti-spyware program called Windows Defender.

The companies that offer free security tools tend to specialise in one particular area so you will need to download and install separate anti-virus, anti-spyware and firewall programs to make sure your computer is fully protected. You will also have to maintain and monitor each one separately as you're unlikely to get the same support that you would receive with a paid-for security suite.

Using anti-virus software

When you first install an anti-virus program, it will automatically run a scan of your computer for viruses. Once completed you can use the program's settings to schedule regular scans and decide what the program should do if it encounters a virus.

In Microsoft Security Essentials, for example, when the first scan is complete, click the **Settings** tab. On the next screen tick the box next to 'Run a schedule scan on my computer (recommended)'. Choose the frequency, time and type of scan you want from the drop-down menu boxes below. Tick the box next to 'Check for the latest virus and spyware definitions before running a scheduled scan'. This will ensure that the software checks for updates before running a scan.

If your computer is at risk from a virus, your anti-virus software will provide an alert and an option to solve the problem. In the case of Microsoft Security Essentials, you will see a red icon on the Home page along with details of the threat. Click the **Clean computer** button and Microsoft Security Essentials will remove the infected file and then do a quick scan for additional malicious software. If you want more information on the alert, you can click the **Show details** link to display the 'Potential threat details' window.

How do I know if my anti-virus software is on?

Most anti-virus programs show they're working by placing a flag or icon in the notification area of your taskbar (bottom-right of the screen). You can also check the anti-virus setting in Window 7's 'Action Center', found in the 'System and Security' section on the 'Control Panel' window.

How can I tell if my computer has a virus?

If your computer becomes slow or unresponsive, or programs and menus start to behave in an unusual way, your computer may be infected by a virus.

How many anti-virus programs should I run?

Just one. Don't install more than one program or security software suite at the same time as two anti-virus programs or two firewalls can conflict with each other. You can, however, use two or more anti-spyware programs, although only one should be set for automatic scanning.

How do I scan for viruses?

In most cases, a Scan option will be available on the main program page. Check the anti-virus program settings for scheduling options so you can set it to run a daily- or weekly-automated scan.

Jargon buster

Trojans A computer virus that disguises itself as an innocent program to entice people to install it. They can allow third parties complete access to you computer.

Worm Similar to a virus, except a worm doesn't need to attach itself to a document and can simply spread via the internet.

How often should I update my anti-virus software?

Daily. Good anti-virus software will do this automatically. In other cases, you may see a message pop-up alerting you when updates are available.

I think my firewall isn't turned on!

By default, most Windows 7 computers will have the Firewall turned on. But if you suspect that it isn't, it is easy to turn the Firewall on.

1 Click **Start**, then click **Control Panel**. In the window that appears, type **firewall** in the search box. Click **Windows Firewall** in the results list. Click **Turn Windows Firewall on or off** in the left panel. You may have to enter your administrator password at this point.

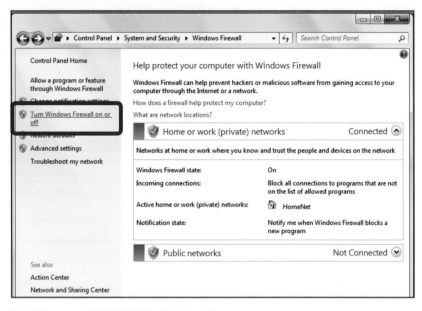

2 Under each of the network locations – such as 'Home or work' – click **Turn on Windows Firewall** for all the locations that you want to protect.

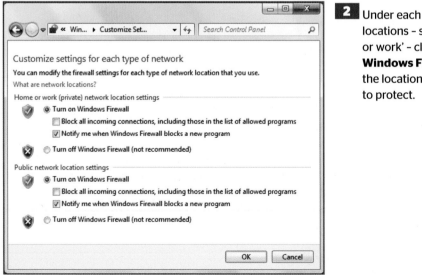

Where to find Windows Defender

To access Windows Defender from Windows, click the **Start** button, point to 'Control Panel' and then click **System and Security**. Type **windows defender** in the search box, then click **Windows Defender** in the list of results.

Performing a manual scan

1 Click **Scan** and Defender will look for spyware. The scan may take a few minutes. You can then ignore, remove or quarantine files.

Setting up an automatic scan

1 To set your computer to run an automatic daily scan, click **Tools** and then click **Options**.

2 Under 'Automatic scanning' tick the 'Automatically scan my computer (recommended)' box, select the frequency, time of day and type of scan you want to run.

3 You can set Windows Defender to automatically remove spyware. In the left pane click **Default actions**. Select **Recommended action based on definitions** for all alert items.

4 Click the **Apply recommended actions** tick box and then click **Save**.

Reinstalling Windows 7

If you need to reinstall Windows 7 back to its original settings because it has a major unfixable problem, then you can either use System Restore to return it to a previous state (see pages 202-3) or reinstall Windows 7 and return your computer to its factory settings.

1 Click **Start**, then click **Control Panel.** Type **recovery** in the 'Control Panel' search box. Click **Restore your computer or reinstall Windows** in the search results.

2 Click **Advanced recovery methods** in the window and then choose one of the following:

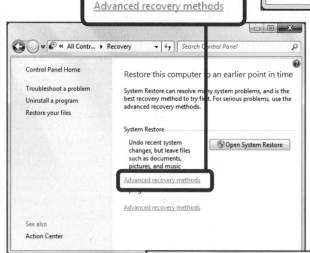

■ **Use a system image you created earlier to recover your computer**. This will restore Windows and some of your personal settings and files, such as photos in the Picture library, from a Backup and Restore disk that you will need to have created earlier (see pages 200-201).

■ **Reinstall Windows (requires Windows installation disc)**. This will reinstall Windows 7 on your computer, but it will not delete any user files. It will delete any programs you have installed since Windows 7 was first installed, so you will need to reinstall these afterwards. A new folder, called 'Windows.old' will be created that stores all the user files so you can reapply settings once Windows 7 has been reinstalled.

BE CAREFUL!

Continuing with reinstalling Windows 7 will delete data from your hard drive, including personal files and settings. Make sure that you have a full backup of valuable information before you continue. See page 198 for advice on backing up your files.

Resources

Jargon buster

Adobe Flash Software that allows your web browser to display animation, video and interactivity on web pages. Commonly used for internet advertising and games.

Adware Software that tracks your web use to determine your interests and deliver relevant adverts.

Anti-spyware Software that prevents and/ or removes spyware.

Anti-virus Software that scans for viruses and removes them from your computer.

Applets A small application, such as a utility program, that performs one or two simple tasks.

Application see Program

Attachment A computer file that is sent along with an email message. It can be any type of software file, and can be opened by the receiver if the appropriate software to view the file attachment is installed or available.

Backup A copy of you files or programs for safekeeping

Bluetooth A type of short-range wireless connection for transferring data between devices.

Bookmarks A collection of favourite websites visited and saved by the user.

Broadband A method of connecting to the Internet via cable or ADSL. Much faster than a dial-up connection.

Browser The software that enables you to view web pages. Often these contain phishing filters.

Browser history A folder, stored by the browser, which contains details of recently visited websites.

Cache The way web browsers store recently accessed pages, images, and other data so they can be displayed rapidly the next time they're requested.

Card reader A device for reading data stored on Memory Cards, such as used by digital cameras.

Case sensitive Most search tools are not case sensitive or only respond to initial capitals, as in proper names. But as capital letters (upper case) retrieve only upper case, it's best to type lower case (no capitals) because lower case will always retrieve upper case letters too.

CD-R/RW Drive A Compact Disc Recordable or Rewritable can record data, images or music files onto blank discs.

Cloud storage Nothing to do with the weather, cloud storage refers to online backup or storage services that host a copy of your files and folders on giant computers known as servers. These are remote from your computer and you can access them via the internet.

Cookie A piece of information sent to a user's web browser by a website. The web browser then returns that information to the website. This is how some websites 'remember' your previous visits.

Control panel A series of dedicated programs than adjust the computer's settings, such as passwords, internet access and accessibility.

CSV file A commonly used way of moving data from one application to another, a Comma Separated Values (CSV) file is a text file that saves data (text and numbers) in an organised fashion. Also known as a Comma Delimited file, when it is opened in a word processing program, each piece of information (value) is shown separated by a comma.

Cursor A cursor is the symbol on the screen that shows you where the next character will appear.

Desktop The main screen you see when you start your computer. From here you can organise and access programs and files.

Dial-up An internet connection via a normal phone line, which is slow compared to broadband.

Download To transfer data from a remote computer to your own computer over the internet.

Driver Software that allows your computer to communicate with other devices, such as a printer.

DVD-R/RW Drive Optical drive that can read and write to DVD discs.

Email client A computer program that manages emails. Emails are stored on your computer and you only need to be connected to the internet to send and receive emails.

External hard drive A storage device that plugs into your PC. Useful for saving copies of important files, or creating additional storage.

File compression The act of reducing the size of one or more files using a special compression program so that they can be more easily stored or transferred across the internet.

File extension The letters that appear after a file name. They show what type of document it is, and what type of program will open it – for example, a Microsoft Word document will end in .doc.

Firewall Software (or hardware) that blocks unwanted communication from, and often to, the internet.

Flash drive see Memory stick

Gif Short for Graphics Interchange Format, Gif is a popular format for image files, with built-in data compression. Commonly used for images on web pages, it's not suitable for printing.

Graphics rendering The computer process of generating an image on screen through the translating of the programming code that describes the image – essentially drawing the image on the screen.

Hard disk The main long-term storage space used by your computer to store data. Also known as a hard drive.

Hard drive see Hard disk

HTML An abbreviation of HyperText Markup Language, the computer programming language that is used to create web pages.

Icon A small picture that represents an object or program.

Identity theft The stealing of someone's personal information to commit fraud using the stolen identity. Criminals use another person's identity to steal money or obtain credit and other benefits.

IMAP Short for Internet message access protocol, IMAP is one of two methods for sending and retrieving email. IMAP stores all your email on a remote mail server, so that you can view email from any location on any computer or device, such as smartphone, that's connected to the internet.

IP ADDRESS An Internet Protocol address (IP address) is a number that identifies a computer or other device on a network (including the internet), making it possible for other computers to find and communicate with it.

Link Short for hyperlink, a link can be either text or an image that lets you jump straight to another webpage when you click on it.

Log in/out To log in or sign in is to provide a username and password to identify yourself to a website. To log out or sign out is to notify the site that you're no longer using it, which will deny you (and other people who might subsequently use your web browser) access to the functions until you log in again.

Lorem ipsum A piece of garbled Latin text that's commonly used as mock-content when creating or testing a template, page layout or font usage.

Malware Malicious software. A generic term for any program that is harmful to your computer, for example, a virus.

Memory stick Small, portable device used to store and transfer data. It plugs into a USB port and is sometimes called a USB key, flash drive or pen drive.

Memory card Removable storage device, which holds images taken with the camera. They come in a variety of sizes and there are several types including Compact Flash, Multimeda and SD cards as well as Sony's Memory Stick format.

Metadata Information stored within a digital file. Most digital cameras store photos with extra information – known as metadata – and includes information such as copyright details or creation date.

MP3 The standard file format for digital music. The attraction of the format is that it is not tied to any one manufacturer in the way that AAC (Apple) and WMA (Microsoft) are.

MP3 player A portable music player that plays digital music.

MsConfig Also know as System Configuration in Windows 7 and Windows Vista, this is is a Microsoft utility that troubleshoots the Windows startup process.

Network A system of communication between two or more computers.

Operating system The software that manages your computer and the environment that programs operate in.

PDF A file that captures the graphics, fonts and formatting of a document, regardless of the application in which it was created.

Phishing A type of email scam where you're tricked into giving away personal details by being directed to a spoof website that resembles the site of an official organisation (a bank, for example).

Pop-up A small window that appears over an item (word or picture) on your computer screen to give additional information.

POP (Post office protocol) A way of allowing an email server (a computer dedicated to delivering email) to 'post' emails to your computer.

Port A computer socket into which you plug equipment.

Processor The main computer chip that controls and carries out the functions of the computer. The better the processor, the more a computer can do in a given amount of time.

Ram The short-term memory of the computer, it holds all running programs.

ReadyBoost A Windows feature that lets you add memory to a system using flash memory, such as a USB drive – to improve performance without having to add additional system memory.

SD card A small media card that stores data – SD cards are used by digital cameras and camcorders to store photos or video.

Security suite A bundle of security programs to protect your PC.

SMTP (Simple mail transfer protocol) A standard internet protocol allowing an email program on your computer to deliver outgoing emails to an online email server (such as a webmail service).

Social networking A way for people to socialise online, typically via a website, such as Facebook or Twitter.

Software A general term for programs used to operate computers and related devices.

Silverlight A free web-browser plug-in that allows you to see video, animation and interactive content on web pages.

Spam Unsolicited junk email.

Spam filter Software or a system that helps to keep spam out of your email inbox.

Spyware Software that secretly installs on your computer and is able to track your internet behaviour and send details to a third party.

System registry A central database used by Windows to store information about user preferences, installed software, hardware and drivers, and other settings needed for the operating system to run correctly.

Tab-delimited file Similar to a CSV file (see page 216), a tab delimited files uses tabs to separate values.

Taskbar The bar running across the bottom of your screen, from where you can open programs and access the main Windows functions.

Toolbar A vertical or horizontal onscreen bar that's made up of small icons that, when clicked, will perform a task.

Trojans A computer virus that disguises itself as an innocent program to entice people to install it. They can allow third parties to have complete access to your computer remotely.

Upload Process of sending files from your computer to the internet.

USB (Universal Serial Bus) A connection technology that allows you to transfer data easily between a computer and a device, such as a camera or printer. USB cables are used to connect devices and are plugged into a USB port on your computer.

USB dongle Any small USB device – such as a USB drive or 3G broadband device – that plugs into the USB port of your laptop.

USB key see Memory stick

Username Also called a login name, screen name, or login, it is a unique name used to identify a person online.

URL (Uniform Resource Locator) A website's 'address'.

Virus A malevolent program that spreads from computer to computer within another program or file.

WAV Sometimes written as WAVE, WAV is short for Waveform Audio File Format as used by Windows audio files. WAV sound files end with in .wav and can be played by nearly all Windows applications that support sound.

Web browser See Browser

Webmail Email accounts accessed through your web browser. Email is not stored locally on your computer.

Webpage Each website on the internet usually has more than one page, these are referred to as webpages. Each webpage has a unique address that you type in to go directly to that page.

Wi-fi A wireless high-speed networking system that can transfer data at high speeds across lots of different devices.

Windows Gadgets A small application that sits on the desktop and performs a simple function, such as displaying the time or the weather.

Worm Similar to a virus, except a worm doesn't need to attach itself to a document and can simply spread via the internet.

Index

About the consultant editor Lynn Wright
Lynn Wright is an editor and journalist with 20 years' experience in writing about computing, technology and digital photography.

Which?

One-to-one computer advice

Which? Computing has a successful online Helpdesk service. The team has a combined experience of over forty years and promises to answer questions within two working days. To date, the team has answered tens of thousands of queries from readers, and there's no PC problem they won't tackle.

As a reader of *Computer Problem Solving Made Easy*, you can now access this indispensable service absolutely free. To submit a question for the Helpdesk*, simply go to www.which.co.uk/computinghelpdesk

Enter your query and, where it asks for a membership number, simply enter the code that you'll find on the page of 'Use the System Repair Disc' in the Essential advice chapter.

*This service is only available online